THE PD'S

Pronunciation Drills for Learners of English

by Edith Crowell Trager
and Sara Cook Henderson

ELS Publications
A Division of W.E.R.A., Inc.
5761 Buckingham Parkway
Culver City, CA 90230

ISBN 0-87789-008-0

Printed in the United States of America

FOREWORD

The purpose of the Pronunciation Drills is to help the foreign students learning English to make automatic the systems of the phonology and morphology of the language. The lessons are based on the Trager-Smith analysis of English.

In the *PD*'s, each vowel, consonant and stress phoneme is drilled alone, in words of ultra-high frequency garnered from the Bell Telephone frequency list, Thorndike, and a supplementary list of our own. The most frequent intonation patterns are also treated. Each phoneme is drilled in contrast with similar phonemes, by means of minimal pairs--pairs of words which differ in one sound only, like *shop* and *chop*, or *live* and *leave*. Short sentences using high-frequency words are given for each point drilled. At the end of the book, English spelling is treated in relation to the phonemic system.

An attempt has been made to introduce the problems in order of importance (importance being determined by the frequency of the item and its effect on intelligibility). Thus, vowels are treated first, since every syllable has one, stress and intonation are treated next, since every word has a stress pattern and every utterance an intonation pattern, and consonants last. There is also an internal order in each category, so that /s, z, t, d, θ, and ð/ are treated first among the consonants, for instance, because of their position in the morphological system of English. However, teachers may often find it more satisfactory to use the lessons in a different order, according to the needs of their class.

A satisfactory way to use the PD's is as follows: In the first section of each lesson (*Words Frequently Used*) the teacher pronounces the words and sentences and if necessary explains the meaning. Next the entire class repeats the words and sentences after the teacher. Then the individual students repeat the words and sentences after the teacher. The amount of individual work done varies according to class level, number of students, and the particular problems of the students.

In using the second section of each lesson (*Words in Contrast*) the teacher should make sure that the students understand that here the concern is entirely with the pronunciation of the words, and not with the meaning. It is also important to be sure that the student can hear the difference between the two sounds being drilled. The teacher repeats the pairs of words in this way:"ship" (pause for class repetition) "chip" (pause for class repetition) "ship, chip". The amount of individual work again varies according to class needs.

After a PD has been practiced thoroughly in class, it should be drilled in the laboratory. Each PD tape lasts for approximately fifteen minutes. Occasional use of the tape recorder which allows the student to record and listen to his own pronunciation is very valuable.

Mrs. Trager and Mrs. Henderson planned both Part 1 and Part 2 of the PD's, with the constant encouragement of the Director of the American Language Center, Dr. A. L. Davis. Mrs. Trager is responsible for the over-all arrangement, and the specific arrangement of each lesson in Part 1, Mrs. Henderson for the specific arrangement of Part 2, and for the revision. They are both indebted to Dr. William Austin for reading the manuscript and giving helpful suggestions, to Mrs. Winifred Jones for her file of morpheme charts, to Miss Sue Hoover, and Dr. Kenneth Croft, and to various other teachers at the American Language Center who have offered helpful criticisms and suggestions.

SELECTED LIST OF SPECIAL PRONUNCIATION PROBLEMS
according to students' native language

V=Vowel(s)
C=Consonant(s)
-/-=Contrasts (between the phonemes on
either side of the bar)

All students: Vowel drills; r, θ/ð; stress and intonation.

Most students: ŋ; final stops; s/z, t/d, w/v, y/j, š/č, l/r; initial and final clusters; polysyllables.

Spanish-speaking students: all the above; b/v, final m/n/ŋ.

Asian students: initial, medial and final l/r; l/r clusters (fl, fr, gl, gr, bl, br, etc.); final clusters, especially Cs, Cz, Ct, Cd.

Arabic: ow, oy, i/e/æ, a/ə/u, i/iy, e/ey, u/uw; p, ŋ, š/j/ž, g/j; clusters.

Burmese: i/iy, e/ey, u/uw; final stops; f/v, l/r; final clusters.

Chinese: all V; b, d, g, v, θ, ð; all final C except n and ŋ; h/š, š/č, j/ž.

French: ə, oy, i/iy, e/ey, u/uw; h, θ, ð, s/t/θ, č/š, j/ž.

German: θ, ð; all voiced finals; p/b, t/θ, d/ð, s/z, w/v, j/y, č/š, n/ŋ, s clusters.

Haitian: same as French, plus final C; y/ž.

Indonesian: oy, i/iy, e/ey, u/uw; θ, ð, š, ž, f, v; final b, d, j, g, ð, z, ž; w/v; clusters.

Iranian: i/e/æ, a/ə, i/iy, e/ey, u/uw, ow/aw; medial ŋ; v/w, s/θ, θ/ð; s clusters; final clusters.

Italian: i/iy, u/uw; h, θ, ð, s/š; initial fl, pl, bl; final clusters; unstressed syllables; stress.

Japanese: all V; unstressed i, u; θ, ð, s/š, f/h, z/ž, t/ts, š/č, w/v, l/r; all clusters.

Korean: i/iy, e/ey, u/uw, oh/ow; all voiced sounds; θ, ð; medial p, t, č, k; p, t, č, k before nasals; final b, d, j, g and spirants; nasals after ð and r; l/r, ŋ/ŋg.

Laotian: same as for Thai, but not l/r.

Polish: ə, long V, diphthongs; θ, ð; w, l; ŋ/ŋg, final w/l; unstressed syllables.

v

Portuguese: h, n, ŋ; final l; final stops; č/j, all clusters; final unstressed syllables.

Spanish: e/ey, i/iy, u/uw, u/ə; final voiced C; b/v, y/j, s/z, s/θ, s/š/č, d; final m/n/ŋ; s clusters; final clusters.

Thai: ə, i/iy, e/ey, u/uw, oh/ow; θ, ð; final voiced stops; l/r, š/č, s/z, v/w, č/j, z/ž.

Turkish: all V; e; ŋ; k, g before e, i; final voiced C; w/v; initial and final clusters.

Vietnamese: i/e, ey, uw, e/æ: initial p; y, r, final voiced C: k, ŋ after u, o, w; š/ž.

TABLE OF CONTENTS

PART I

GROUP I

GROUP II

GROUP III

GROUP XI

GROUP XVI

The relative positions of the tongue in the simple vowel-sounds are shown in Diagram 1. Note that in the complex vowel-sounds, the tongue moves from a simple vowel position (1) upward and front in the case of /y/ (Diagram 2), (2) towards the center in the case of /h/ (Diagram 3), and (3) upward and backward in the case of /w/ (Diagram 4).

A. Simple Vowels

	Front (unrounded)	Central (unrounded)	Back (rounded)
High	i p*i*t	ɨ judg*e*s	u p*u*t
Mid	e p*e*t	ə j*u*dges	o (November)
Low	æ p*a*t	a p*o*t	ɔ (sorry)

Diagram 1

B. Complex nuclei (vowel plus glide):

Diagram 2	Diagram 3	Diagram 4
y-glide	h-glide	w-glide

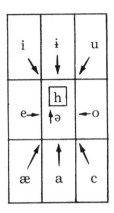
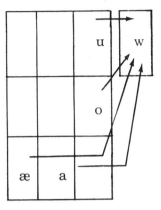

see /síy/	ear /íhr/	who /húw/
say /séy/	air /éhr/	hoe /hów/
sigh /sáy/	(baa /bǽh/)	how /háw/ or /hǽw/
soy /sóy/	(bird /bɨ́hrd/)	
	furred /fə́hrd/)	
	bar /báhr/	
	sure /šúhr/	
	shore /šóhr/	
	(war /wɔ́hr/)	

PART I

GROUP I

Vowels / i e æ /

Pronunciation Drill 1

1. The Vowel / i/

Words frequently used

Practice the following common words containing the "short *i* sound" /i/, as in *pit*.

pit	give	his	big
it	live	been	sing
is	15, 50	think	hit
in	16, 60	minute	million
him	will	sit	wish
with	which	women	Miss
this	did	busy	Mister
thing	didn't	business	Mrs.

Sentences

1. This is it.
2. Miss Mills thinks it's big.
3. Which children did it?
4. Is it his?

2. The Vowel /e/

Words frequently used

Practice the following common words containing the "short *e* sound" /e/, as in *pet*.

pet	when	F, L, M, N, S, X	Wednesday
get	weather	ten	February
let	dead	eleven	September
yes	sell	twelve	December
them	any	7, 17, 70	tell
men	many	well	then
says	very	better	again
said	yet	best	friend

1

Sentences

5. Let's get Ed a pen.
6. Many men said yes.
7. When did Ted send the letter?
8. The weather's better in September.

3. *The Vowel* /æ/

Words frequently used

Practice the following common words containing the "short *a* sound" /æ/, as in *pat.*

(Some speakers of English have the sound /æ/ in words like "pat, clap, back, catch" and the other words in the first and second columns; they may have different sounds, which we write /æh/ or /eh/ in words like "man, bad, cab", and in other words in the third and fourth columns. Other speakers of English have the same vowel-sound in all the words below. Both pronunciations are correct.)

pat	back	man	can
at	that	ask	bad
as	catch	glad	last
has	Saturday	cab	laugh
have	perhaps	understand	half
had	matter	bag	class

Sentences

9. Jack can't understand that.
10. That man ran after his hat.
11. Half the class has had it.
12. Has Dad had a nap?

4. *Vowels* / i e /

Words in contrast

Concentrate only on the pronunciation of these words.

Now you will hear some pairs of words which differ only in having the "short *i* sound" /i/, as in *pit*, or the "short *e* sound" /e/, as in *pet.*

pit pet	miss mess	sit set
pick peck	rid red	nick neck
Sid said	bit bet	lid led
hid head	knit net	bliss bless
din den	win when	Jim gem
string strength	imminent eminent	did dead

pig peg
mitt met
pin pen
since sense
in N

Sentences

13. This weather is getting better.
14. Then again, I think it's best this way.
15. Let's get busy, men.

5. *Vowels / e æ /*

Words in contrast

Now you will hear some pairs of words which differ only in having the "short e sound" /e/, as in *pet*, or the "short a sound /æ/, as in *pat*.

pet pat	mess mass	dead Dad	set sat
peck pack	neck knack	beg bag	bed bad
said sad	met mat	net gnat	led lad
then than	merry marry	very vary	M am
lend land	spend spanned	N an	

Sentences

16. Pass the jelly, Edna.
17. Get back exactly at midnight, Miss Smith.
18. Let's ask Dad's friends.

6. Vowels / i e æ /

Words in contrast

Now you will hear contrasts between the three sounds you have been practicing: /i/, /e/, and /æ/. There are conventional names for these three sounds. *Repeat them.*

Conventional Name	Sound	Examples
"the short *a* sound"	/ æ /	pat
"the short *e* sound"	/ e /	pet
"the short *i* sound"	/ i /	pit

Each of the following groups of words includes one word with one of the "short *a* sounds" /æ/ or /eh/, another word with "the short *e* sound" /e/, and a third word with "the short *i* sound" /i/.

pit pet pat	pat pet pit
sit set sat	set sit sat
lid led lad	led lad lid
nick neck knack	knack nick neck
knit net gnat	gnat knit net
bin Ben ban	Ben bin ban
mirror merry marry	miss mess mass

did dead Dad	mass mess miss
pick peck pack	dead did Dad
mitt met mat	pick pack peck
is says has	mat met mitt
pin pen pan	has says is
dribble rebel rabble	in N an

Review sentences

Review sentences 1-18, which you have practiced. Sentences 19-22 have words with all the sounds you have been studying.

A. Sentences with / i /

    1. This is it.
    2. Miss Mills thinks it's big.
    3. Which children did it?
    4. Is it his?

B. Sentences with / e /

    5. Let's get Ed a pen.
    6. Many men said yes.
    7. When did Ted send the letter?
    8. The weather's better in September.

C. Sentences with / æ / or /eh/

    9. Jack can't understand that.
   10. That man ran after his hat.
   11. Half the class has had it.
   12. Has Dad had a nap?

D. Sentences with / i / and / e /

   13. This weather is getting better.
   14. Then again, I think it's best this way.
   15. Let's get busy, men.

E. Sentences with / e / and / æ /

   16. Pass the jelly, Edna.
   17. Get back exactly at midnight,
       Miss Smith.
   18. Let's ask Dad's friends.

F. Sentences with / i / , / e /, and / æ /

   19. Bill has seven children.
   20. When did Ann tell him?
   21. Has Ed been pretty busy?
   22. The women met last Saturday.

Vowels /æ a ɔ ə/

Pronunciation Drill 3

1. *Vowels /a ɔ/*

Words frequently used

There are many regional variations in the pronunciation of the "short o sounds". A large number of Americans use the /a/ vowel sound in the words in Column 1 and Column 2 below, and the /ɔ/ vowel sound in the words in Column 3 and Column 4. Imitate your teacher's pronunciation.

Practice the following common words containing the "short o sounds" the /a/ and /ɔ/, as in *pot, dog*.

1	2	3	4
pot	hot	dog*	water*
not	dollar	chalk	call
got	October	gone	long
box	job	tall	lost
doctor	o'clock	often*	coffee*
a lot	watch	song	off*

Some Americans use / a / in these words.

Sentences

1. The clock stopped.
2. It's not a lot.
3. Tom got the job in October.
4. The coffee's strong.
5. Ed lost his dog.
6. Is the song very long?

2. *The Vowel / ə /*

Words frequently used

Practice the following common words containing the "short u sound" /ə/, as in *putt* (a golf stroke).

putt	a cup	was*	double
up	the cup	from	trouble
us	some	Sunday	touch
but	of	Monday	mother
under	month	money	brother
sun	another	son	love
much	does	above	one
just	done	enough	won
one hundred	come	young	number

Some Americans use /a/ in this word.

Sentences

7. The sun comes up at seven.
8. Mother loves the summer months.
9. Does Sunday come before Monday?
10. Hasn't Gus won enough money?

3. *Vowels / æ a ɔ /*

Words in contrast

Now you will hear some pairs of words which differ only in their vowel-sounds: the "short *a* sound" /æ/, as in *lack* or /eh/ as in *mass*; the "short *o* sound" /a/, as in *lock*, or /ɔ/ as in *moss*.

pat	pot	mass	moss
map	mop	knack	knock
sad	sod	cat	cot
hat	hot	cab	cob
nab	knob	hag	hog
rang	wrong	passable	possible

lack	lock	bass	boss
lag	log	bag	bog
gnat	not	rat	rot
add	odd	jab	job
had	hod	tang	tong
sang	song	impossible	impassable

7

Sentences

11. I want a *ham* sandwich–not a *hot* sandwich.
12. Has Ann got a job?
13. What had Jack's boss wanted?
14. Bob got back at one o'clock.

4. *Vowels* / ə a ɔ /

Words in contrast

Now you will hear some pairs of words which differ only in
their vowel sounds; if the vowel-letter is *u*, the sound is / ə /,
as in *putt, but*; if the vowel-letter is *o*, the sound is /a or ɔ/,
as in *pot* or *dog*.

pot	putt	lock	luck	hot	hut	rot	rut
moss	muss	boss	bus	dog	dug	long	lung
song	sung	wrong	rung	lost	lust	bossed	bust
scoff	scuff			cop	cup		

Sentences

15. John's sorry, but he doesn't want to come.
16. The doctor does *not* come from Florida.
17. Bob mustn't touch the hundred-dollar watch.
18. Was John's *younger* brother in trouble?

Pronunciation Drill 4

5. *Vowels* /æ a ɔ ə/

Words in contrast

Now you will hear some pairs of words which differ in their
vowel-sounds: the "short *a* sound" /æ/, as in *lack*, or /eh/,
as in *mass*; the "short *o* sound" /a/, as in *pot*, or /ɔ/, as in
dog; the "short *u* sound" /ə/, as in *putt*.

pat	pot	putt	blander	blonder	blunder
last	lost	lust	lack	lock	luck
sadden	sodden	sudden	gnat	knot	nut

mass	moss	muss
stack	stock	stuck
rang	wrong	rung

battle	bottle	rebuttal
bass	boss	bus
sang	song	sung

Sentences

19. When does Tom get back?
20. Tom gets back on Monday.
21. Does Kansas get as hot as it gets here?
22. Kansas got as hot as Washington, last summer.

Review sentences

Review the sentences which you practiced in PD 3 and 4.

A. Sentences with / a / or / ɔ /
 1. The clock stopped.
 2. It's not a lot.
 3. Tom got the job in October.
 4. The coffee's strong.
 5. Ed lost his dog.
 6. Is the song very long?

B. Sentences with / ə /
 7. The sun comes up at seven.
 8. Mother loves the summer months.
 9. Does Sunday come before Monday?
 10. Hasn't Gus won enough money?

C. Sentences with / æ / and / a / or / ɔ /
 11. I want a *ham* sandwich—not a *hot* sandwich.
 12. Has Ann got a job?
 13. What had Jack's boss wanted?
 14. Bob got back at one o'clock.

9

D. Sentences with / a / or / ɔ / and / ə /

15. John's sorry, but he doesn't want to come.
16. The doctor does *not* come from Florida.
17. Bob mustn't touch the hundred-dollar watch.
18. Was John's *younger* brother in trouble?

E. Sentences with / æ /, / a / or / ɔ / and / ə /

19. When does Tom get back?
20. Tom gets back on Monday.
21. Does Kansas get as hot as it gets here?
22. Kansas got as hot as Washington, last summer.

The Vowel / u / And A Review of the Short Vowel Sounds

Pronunciation Drill 5

1. The Vowel / u /

Words frequently used

Practice the following common words containing the "short oo sound", /u/, as in *put*.

put	foot	wood	wouldn't	pull
good	could	wool	cook	look
book	should	couldn't	woolen	took
woman	would	shouldn't	push	full

Sentences

1. Would this be a good book?
2. He shouldn't have stood on that foot.
3. She took the book and put it away.
4. Look at that pretty woman.

2. Vowels /u ə/

Words in contrast

Now you will hear some pairs of words which differ in their vowel sounds: the "short *u* sound" /ə/, as in *putt*; the "short *oo* sound" /u/, as in *put*.

putt	put	luck	look	cud	could	buck	book
tuck	took	stud	stood	crux	crooks	put	putt
look	luck	could	cud	book	buck	took	tuck
		stood	stud	crooks	crux		

Sentences

5. She couldn't have stood the sight of blood.
6. Should one push it up, or pull it down?
7. The woman wouldn't come up.
8. Good luck!

3. Vowels /u ə a/

Words in contrast

Now you will hear some groups of words which differ in their vowel sounds: the "short *oo* sound" /u/, as in *put*; the "short *u* sound" /ə/, as in *putt*; the "short *o* sound" /a/, as in *pot*.

Words with / u /:   put good look could book shook
Words with / ə / :   putt gun luck cud buck shuck
Words with / a / :   pot god lock cod bock shock

pot putt put   god good gun   look lock luck
could cud cod   buck bock book   shuck shook shock

Sentences

9. The book was *not* good.
10. Would you look at Bobby's foot, Mother?
11. The woman put the books back in the box.
12. The parking lot was full.

4. The Short Vowel Sounds

Review

Here is a complete list of the short vowel sounds in one type of standard American speech. *Listen* when the speaker says, "say the short *i* sound, as in *pit*", *then repeat.*

Conventional Name	Phonemic Symbol	Key Words
the short *i* sound	/ i /	pit
the short *e* sound	/ e /	pet
the short *a* sound	/ æ /, / eh /	pat, man
the short *o* sound	/ a /, / ɔ /	pot, dog
the short *u* sound	/ ə /	putt, but
the short *oo* sound	/ u /	put, good

Be sure you can pronounce the following groups of key words correctly.

pat pet pit   pet pit pat   pet pat pot pat pot putt

pot putt pat pot putt put put pot putt pit pet pat

pot putt put put putt pot   pat pet pit

Be sure you can pronounce the following groups of words correctly.

miss mess mass   mass moss muss   miss mass muss
mess moss mass   mass mess miss   miss moss muss
din Dan Don   Dan den din Don dun   pill pal pull
but bat bottle   bat bet bit bottle but
back buck book back beck bicker buck book

Pronunciation Drill 6

5. *Vowels* / ɔh ah /

Words frequently used

Practice the following common words containing the "*aw* sound" / ɔh/, as in *saw*.

saw	call	because	brought
Shaw	fall	applause	thought
straw	small	caught	walk
awful	Paul	ought	daughter
all	pause	bought	cough

(Turn back to page 6 and review the words in Columns 3 and 4, and the remarks in the paragraph above. In the words "dog, long, off", and in other words spelled with *o*, many Americans do not use the vowel sound of short duration, /ɔ/, they use a similar vowel sound of longer duration, written here /ɔh/. This is the "*aw* sound" which you practiced in the words listed above, "saw, law", etc.

There are a great many regional variations in the pronunciation of the "short *o* sounds" and the "*aw* sound". Imitate your teacher's pronunciation.)

Sentences

13. I thought I saw Paul.
14. Has Mr. Hall taught law?
15. All Shaw thought of was applause.
16. We ought to walk and talk together.

6. *Vowels* /ɔh ah/

Words in contrast

Now you will hear some pairs of words which differ in their vowel sounds: one word has the "*aw* sound" /ɔh/, as in *saw*; the other word has the "short *o* sound" /a or ɔ/, as in *pot*, *dog*.

coffer	cougher	nod	gnawed	cod	cawed	odd	awed
cot	caught	Poll	Paul	tot	taught	not	naught
knotty	naughty	rot	wrought	chock	chalk	stock	stalk
yon	yawn	Oz	awes	clod	clawed	Don	dawn

The /ah/ sound in contrast with /a/ and /ɔh/

A great many speakers of English in the Eastern United States have a vowel sound that is like /a/, but is of longer duration. The phonemic writing for this sound is /ah/ and the most usual spellings are *-a* and *-ah* at the end of a word, and the *a* in *-alm*.

Ah! Shah Pa Ma spa calm palm psalm father

/a/ - /ah/ contrasts

bomb	balm	comma	calmer	insomnia	psalm
pod	Pa'd	bother	father		

/ah/ - /ɔh/ contrasts

Ah!	awe	Shah	Shaw	Ma	maw	spa	spawn
Pa	pawn	Pa's	pause				

If your teacher says words like *bomb* and *balm* alike, imitate his pronunciation. Both types of pronunciation are correct.

14

7. Vowels /u ə a ɔh/

Review sentences

Review sentences 1-16 which you studied in PD 5 and in PD 6. Practice sentences 17-20, which have words with all the sounds you have been studying.

A. Sentences with /u/

   1. Would this be a good book?
   2. He shouldn't have stood on that foot.
   3. She took the book and put it away.
   4. Look at that pretty woman.

B. Sentences with / ə / and / u /

   5. She couldn't have stood the sight of blood.
   6. Should one push it up, or pull it down?
   7. The woman wouldn't come up.
   8. Good luck!

C. Sentences with / u / and / ə / and / a /

   9. The book was *not* good.
  10. Would you look at Bobby's foot, Mother?
  11. The woman put the books back in the box.
  12. The parking lot was full.

D. Sentences with /ɔh/

  13. I thought I saw Paul.
  14. Has Mr. Hall taught law?
  15. All Shaw thought of was applause.
  16. We ought to walk and talk together.

E. Sentences with /u, ə, a, ɔh/

  17. Would Paul and Don be fond of one another?
  18. The song was good.
  19. Joe Shaw should call up his father.
  20. What book would Dr. Davis suggest?

GROUP IV
Complex Vowels /iy ey ay oy /

Pronunciation Drill 7

1. The Complex Vowel / iy /

Words frequently used

Practice the following common words containing the "long *e* sound" /iy/, as in *see*.

see	he	week	maybe
B, C, D, E	she	meet	need
G, P, T, V, Z	we	evening	complete
three	these	please	keep
be	mean	seem	people
me	believe	the (elephant)	leave

Sentences

1. Keep these three for me, please.
2. He sees me three evenings a week.
3. These people seem to believe me.

2. The Complex Vowel /ey/

Words frequently used

Practice the following common words with the "long *a* sound" /ey/, as in *say*.

say	May	place	same
A, J, K, H	may	wait	name
8, 18, 80	way	weight	vacation
ate	eight	make	stay
they	take	maybe	lane
April	neighbor	rain	pay

Sentences

4. They say they'll take a vacation.
5. Eight days in April, and eighteen in May.
6. The rain in Spain stays mainly in the plain.

3. *The Complex Vowel* /ay/

Words frequently used

Practice the following common words containing the "long *i* sound" /ay/, as in *sigh*.

sigh	like	Friday	night
I, Y	my	July	eye
5	mine	all right	fine
9, 19, 90	time	write	by
hi	child	why	buy
high	might	nice	good-bye

Sentences

7. I'd like to buy a nylon tie.
8. My child likes ice cream.
9. Why arrive at five to nine?
10. I'll try to find time by Friday.

4. *The Complex Vowel* /oy/

Words frequently used

Practice the following common words containing the "*oy* sound" /oy/, as in *boy*.

boy	noise	joy	enjoy
choice	noisy	join	boil
toy	coin	Hoyt	avoid
annoy	oil	Freud	oyster

Sentences

11. Roy's enjoying his toys.
12. The boys are rather noisy.

Review the names of the sounds you have been studying in PD 7. There are conventional names for the sounds /iy/ and /ey/ and /ay/. We will call /oy/ the "*oy* sound" since it is almost always spelled *oy* as in *boy*, or *oi* as in *choice* or *noisy*.

Say the conventional names of the other complex vowels, and the key words.

	Phonemic Symbol	Conventional Name	Key Words
1.	/ey/	the long *a* sound	lake, say
2.	/iy/	the long *e* sound	leak, see
3.	/ay/	the long *i* sound	like, sigh

Pronunciation Drill 8

5. *The Complex Vowels* /iy ey ay oy/

Words in contrast

Now you will hear some pairs of words which differ in their vowel sounds: one word has the "long *e* sound" /iy/, as in *see*; the other word has the "long *a* sound" /ey/, as in *say*.

Pete	pate	seat	sate	read	raid	Mead	made
E	A	grease	Grace	lease	lace	seen	sane
mean	main	reek	rake	seek	sake	deem	dame
seem	same	fade	feed	swayed	Swede	slave	sleeve

Sentences

13. We eat steak once a week, these days.
14. She always takes the street car from the station.
15. The "ABCs" means "the alphabet".

6. Complex Vowels /ay oy/

Words in contrast

Now you will hear some pairs of words which differ in their vowel sounds: one word has the "long *i* sound" /ay/, as in *sigh*; the other word has the "*oy* sound" /oy/, as in *boy*.

try	Troy	buys	boys	fried	Freud	rise	Roy's
sigh	soy	rye	Roy	I'll	oil	tie	toy
file	foil	kind	coined	pies	poise	vied	void
line	loin	vice	voice	quite	quoit	trite	Detroit
implies	employs			implied	employed		

Sentences

16. I like boiled rice and soy sauce.
17. I sang "What kind of a noise annoys an oyster".

7. Complex Vowels /iy ey ay oy/

Words in contrast

Now you will hear some groups of words which differ in their vowel sounds. Each word in the group has one of the four following sounds: the "long *e* sound" /iy/, as in *see*; the "long *a* sound" /ey/, as in *say*; the "long *i* sound" /ay/, as in *sigh*; the "*oy* sound" /oy/, as in *soy*.

see	say	sigh	soy
tree	tray	try	Troy
style	stale		
poi	pie	pay	pea
join	Jane	Jean	
soy	sigh	see	say
Troy	try	tree	tray

A	E	I	
grain	green	groin	
toil	tile	tail	teal
B	bay	by	boy
steel	stale	style	
peas	pays	poise	
cane	keen	coin	
see	say	soy	sigh

Sentences

18. He's my baby boy.
19. Has he tried to read James Joyce?
20. My neighbors seem to be nice people.

8. *Complex Vowels* /iy ey ay oy/

Review sentences

Review the sentences you practiced in PD 7 and PD 8.

A. Sentences with /iy/

1. Keep these three for me, please.
2. He sees me three evenings a week.
3. These people seem to believe me.

B. Sentences with /ey/

4. They say they'll take a vacation.
5. 8 days in April and 18 in May.
6. The rain in Spain stays mainly in the plain.

C. Sentences with /ay/

7. I'd like to buy a nylon tie.
8. My child likes ice cream.
9. Why arrive at five to nine?
10. I'll try to find time by Friday.

D. Sentences with /oy/

11. Roy's enjoying his toys.
12. The boys are rather noisy.

E. Sentences with /iy ey ay oy/

13. We eat steak once a week, these days.
14. She always takes the street car from the station.
15. The "ABCs" means "the alphabet".
16. I like boiled rice and soy sauce.
17. I sang "What kind of a noise annoys an oyster".
18. He's my baby boy.
19. Has he tried to read James Joyce?
20. My neighbors seem to be nice people.

20

Vowels /i iy e ey/

Pronunciation Drill 9

1. *Vowels* /i iy/

Words in contrast

This is a very important section. Now you will hear some pairs of words which differ in their vowel sounds. The first word has the "short *i* sound" /i/, as in *live*; the second word has the "long *e* sound" /iy/, as in *leave*.

pit	Pete	live	leave	rid	read	sin	seen
sick	seek	sit	seat	chip	cheap	gyp	jeep
slip	sleep	ship	sheep	lip	leap	fit	feet
grits	greets	mitt	meet	hit	heat	dip	deep

Sentences

1. Potato chips are cheap.
2. Did they fit his feet?
3. Please sit in this seat.
4. I leave the house where I live at five o'clock.
5. Did he say "living" or "leaving"?

2. *Vowels* /iy i/

Words in contrast

Now you will hear some pairs of words which differ in their vowel sounds. The first word has the "long *e* sound" /iy/, as in *leave*; the second word has the "short *i* sound" /i/, as in *live*.

leave	live	eat	it	deed	did	ease	is
cheek	chicken	lead	lid	he'd	hid	tease	'tis
he's	his	we'll	will	green	grin	bean	bin
Gene	gin	feel	fill	meal	mill	these	this
steal	still	kneel	nil	deep	dip	peat	pit

Sentences

6. He's been eating his meals at the mill.
7. Is the steel strike still on?
8. Which of these women did he see?
9. She didn't meet the three children—she missed them.
10. Is it easy?

3. *Vowels* /e ey/

Words in contrast

This is a very important section. Now you will hear some pairs of words which differ in their vowel sounds. The first word has the "short *e* sound" /e/, as in *let*; the second word has the "long *a* sound" /ey/, as in *late*.

pet	pate	let	late	debt	date	red	raid
bet	bait	met	mate	pen	pain	den	Dane
led	laid	wet	wait	get	gate	Ed	aid
Ned	neighed	pepper	paper	wreck	rake	ebb	Abe
fed	fade	bread	braid	west	waste	special	spatial

Sentences

11. They get ten days' vacation.
12. On what date was the debt paid?
13. Your weight is greater when you're wet.
14. Did they say "pepper" or "paper"?

4. *Vowels* /ey e/

Words in contrast

Now you will hear some pairs of words which differ in their vowel sounds. The first word has the "long *a* sound" /ey/, as in *late*; the second word has the "short *e* sound" /e/, as in *let*.

late	let	main	men	age	edge	wade	wed
stayed	stead	wage	wedge	taste	test	chased	chest
Yale	yell	phase	fez	lace	less	tale	tell
James	gems	sale	sell	quail	quell	waste	west
		spatial	special	aches	X		

Sentences

15. They went to bed late.
16. Jane said they'd already met her.
17. Did she take the dress with less lace?
18. They stayed instead of us.

5. *Vowels* /i iy e ey/

Review sentences

Review sentences 1-18 which you have practiced in PD 9. Practice sentences 17-20, which have words with all the sounds you have been studying.

A. Sentences with /i/ and /iy/

1. Potato chips are cheap.
2. Did they fit his feet?
3. Please sit in this seat.
4. I leave the house where I live at five o'clock.
5. Did he say "live" or "leave"?
6. He's been eating his meals at the mill.
7. Is the steel strike still on?
8. Which of these women did he see?
9. She didn't meet the three children— she missed them.
10. Is it easy?

B. Sentences with /e/ and /ey/

11. They get ten days' vacation.
12. On what date was the debt paid?
13. Your weight is greater when you're wet.
14. Did they say "pepper" or "paper"?
15. They went to bed late.
16. Jane said they'd already met her.
17. Did she take the dress with less lace?
18. They stayed instead of us.

C. Sentences with /i, iy, e, ey/

19. Will we stay? Yes, we'll stay.
20. They said we might get rain this evening.
21. Did they feel better?
22. They feel better than they felt yesterday.

GROUP VI

Complex Vowels /aw ow uw/

Pronunciation Drill 10

1. The Complex Vowel /aw/

Words frequently used

Practice the following common words with the "*ou* sound" /aw/, as in *house.*

house	power	south	mouth
out	down	cow	proud
hour	doubt	towel	around
our	now	found	ounce
noun	town	sound	pound
about	mouse	thousand	amount
how	cloudy	ground	round

Sentences

1. *Around* and *about* are not nouns.
2. I doubt that he's downtown.
3. How much is a pound of ground round? (steak)

NOTE: Many Americans say /æw/ instead of /aw/, and find the latter sound artificial.

2. The Complex Vowel /ow/

Words frequently used

Practice the following common words containing the "long *o* sound" /ow/, as in *know.*

know	go	close	Ohio
O	so	clothes	show
no	old	home	both
nose	don't	whole	Oklahoma
coat	won't	telephone	told
November	over	moment	only
hold	those	chose	though

Sentences

4. Rose and Joan don't know yet.
5. Oh, did Joe go home?
6. Both those cars are pretty old.

3. The Complex Vowel /uw/

Words frequently used

Practice the following common words containing the "long *oo* sound" /uw/, as in *two*.

too	soon	prove	shoe
two (2)	who	proof	through
to	whom	choose	soup
do	whose	spoon	group
afternoon	food	loose	tooth
you	move	lose	blue

Sentences

7. Do you have a loose tooth?
8. I'm moving to another room this afternoon.
9. Whose group do you belong to?

4. The Complex Vowel /uw/

Words frequently used

The words listed below, like the words in 3, have the /uw/ sound, but when it is spelled with the letter *u*, it is conventionally named the "long *u* sound". The letter *u* also represents the sounds /yuw/, and the conditions under which the /y/ sound is present before /uw/ are explained below in the *Note*, and illustrated in 5.

Practice the following common words containing the "long *u* sound" /uw/, as in *rule*, or /yuw/, as in *use*, *few*.

rule	knew	excuse me	suit
Q, U	news	music	juice
June	beauty	fruit	use (n.)
July	beautiful	review	use (v.)
Tuesday	usually	human	used to

25

10. We used to have quite a few arguments about music.
11. Ruth had some fruit juice in her room.
12. Who will tell the students the news?

NOTE: Read This With Your Teacher's Help:

Many Americans pronounce "long *u*" thus:
/yuw/ - initially, and after /b f m p v/ and /k g h/;
/uw/ - after the other consonant sounds, /č d j l n r s š θ z/.

Another large number of speakers of English, particularly in the American South, have two types of "long *u*" distributed thus:
/yuw/ - initially, after /b f m p v/ and /k g h/ and /d l n s t/;
/uw/ - after the remaining consonant sounds, /č j r š θ z/.

This means that words like *Tuesday*, *new*, and *suit* are pronounced with either the /uw/ sound or the /yuw/ sound, depending on the region.

Some other speakers have a sound we write /ɨw/ after all the consonant sounds, in all words with the "long *u*" sound. These regional variations are all acceptable. Imitate your teacher's pronunciation.

5. *The Sounds* /uw yuw/

Words in contrast

Now you will practice some words which have the sound /uw/: either the "long *oo* sound" as in *too*, or the type of "long *u* sound" as in *rule*; and the sound /yuw/, the other type of "long *u* sound" as in *use* and *few*.

In the words in Column 1 below, all speakers use /uw/; in the words in Column 2 speakers of English use /uw/ or /yuw/ according to the part of the country they come from; in the words in Column 3, all speakers use /yuw/.

1 /uw/ oo, o u, ew (after /č j r/)	2 /(y)uw/ u, ew (after /d l n s tθ)	3 /yuw/ u and ew (initially, and after other consonants)
too chew	Tuesday	use music
do June	due	pupil excuse
soon juice	new	beauty argue
who rule	enthusiasm	few human
zoo true	student	review usually

It follows that some speakers, but not all, have a contrast in the following few pairs of words:

do due   gnu knew   too Tuesday loot lute

All speakers have a contrast in pairs like the following.

who hue	whose hues	who'll Hugh'll	whom Hume
coo Q	fool fuel	pooh pew	coot cute
	moo mew	mood mewed	

The important thing to remember when you have a word with a "long u sound" is this:

Pronounce "long u" as /yuw/ at the beginning of a word and after B, C, F, G, H, M, P, and V.

6. Complex Vowels /aw ow/

Words in contrast

Now you will hear some pairs of words which differ in their vowel sounds: the first word has the "*ou* sound" /aw/, as in *house*; the second word has the "long *o* sound" /ow/, as in *know*.

sow so	noun known	now no	now's knows
how hoe	blouse blows	loud load	scowled scold
	rouse rose	out oat(meal)	

7. *Vowels* /ow ɔh/

Words in contrast

Now you will hear some pairs of words whih differ in their vowel sounds: the first has the "long *o* sound" /ow/, as in *know*; the second word has the "*aw* sound" /ɔh/, as in *saw*.

so saw	low law	oat(meal) ought	boat bought
coat caught	woke walk	coal call	cold called
toll tall	choke chalk	owe awe	ode awed
mode Maude	oaf off	pose paws	close clause
joe jaw	goes gauze	phone fawn	row raw
droll drawl	coast cost	scroll scrawl	slow slaw
	loan lawn	hole hall	

Sentences

13. A local phone call costs ten cents.
14. Now's the time to show us how.
15. Do cows cause tuberculosis?
16. Now Paul, drive downtown slowly.

8. *Vowels* /aw ɔh/

Words in contrast

The "*ou* sound" /aw/, as in *house*, and the "*aw* sound" /ɔh/, as in *saw*, are not at all similar in sound. Occasionally, however, there is confusion between /aw/ and /ɔh/, partly because of the complexity of the English spelling system.

Now you will hear some pairs of words which differ only in their vowel sounds: the first word has the "*ou* sound" /aw/ as in *house*; the second word has the "*aw* sound" /ɔh/, as in *saw*.

sow*	saw	cloud	clawed	fowl	fall
allow	a law	bout	bought	cow	caw
mouse	moss	loud	laud	cows	cause
tout	taught	souse**	sauce	pound	pawned
brown	brawn	down	dawn	row	raw
sows	saws	louse	loss	howl	hall
found	fawned				

*'female swine', /saw/
**Some Americans say /sawz/ instead of /saws/.

9. *Vowels* /aw ow uw/

Words in contrast

Say the conventional names of the complex vowels /aw ow uw/, and then the key words.

Phonemic Symbol	Conventional Name	Key Words
1. /aw/	the *ou* sound	house, now
2. /ow/	the long *o* sound	hope, coat, no
3. /uw/	the long *oo* sound	soon, too, do
4. /uw/ or /yuw/	the long *u* sound	rule, use, few

We have used the symbol /(y)uw/ as a cover symbol to mean the sound /uw/ whether or not it was preceded by the /y/ sound, and whether it was represented in the spelling by *oo*, by *u*, or by some other letters.

Now you will hear some groups of words which differ only in their vowel sounds: one of each group of three words has the "*ou* sound" /aw/, as in *house*; another word has the "long *o* sound" /ow/, as in *hope*; the other word has the "long *u* sound" /(y)uw/, as in *rule* or *use*.

new	no	now	road	rude	rowed
whose	hose	house(v.)	sues	sews	sows

sue	so	sow	who	hoe	how
mow	moo	(hay) mow	ruse	rose	rouse

Sentences

17. Who drove you downtown?
18. I doubt that you know the rules.
19. Do you know how to get to school?
20. *Food* and *nose* are nouns.

Pronunciation Drill 12

10. *Vowels* /u uw/

Words in contrast

Now you will hear some pairs of words which differ in their vowel sounds: the first word has the "short *oo* sound" /u/, as in *put* and *good*; the second word has the "long *oo* sound" /uw/, as in *too*.

pull pool	full fool	stood stewed	wood wooed
look Luke	could cooed	should shoed	hood who'd
book rebuke	soot suit	foot refute	put impute
Toots toots	look leukemia	wooden wound	

You have already studied the "short *oo* sound" /u/. Although this sound does not occur in very many words, the words in which it *does* occur are very frequently used.

> put good book woman foot could should would wood wool took look stood push pull full

Sentences

21. Would some good food put you
    in a good mood?
22. Ruth should move to a *good* rooming house.

11. *Vowels* /aw ow uw (y)uw/

Review Sentences

Review the sentences you practiced in PD 10, 11, and 12.

A. Sentences with /aw/

1. *Around* and *about* are not nouns.
2. I doubt that he's downtown.
3. How much is a pound of ground round?
   (steak)

B. Sentences with /ow/

4. Rose and Joan don't know yet.
5. Oh, did Joe go home?
6. Both those cars are pretty old.

C. Sentences with /uw/

7. Do you have a loose tooth?
8. I'm moving to another room this afternoon.
9. Whose group do you belong to?

D. Sentences with /(y)uw/

10. We used to have quite a few argu-
    ments about music.
11. Ruth has some fruit juice in her room.
12. Who will tell the students the news?

E. Sentences with /aw ow uw (y)uw/

13. A local phone call costs ten cents.
14. Now's the time to show us how.
15. Do cows cause tuberculosis?
16. Now, Paul, drive downtown slowly.
17. Who drove you downtown?
18. I doubt that you know the rules.
19. Do you know how to get to school?
20. *Food* and *nose* are nouns.
21. Would some good food put you in a good mood?
22. Ruth should move to a *good* rooming house.

GROUP VII

Vowels Before R*

Pronunciation Drill 13

1. The Sound /ihr/

Words frequently used

Practice the following common words containing the "long e-r sound "/ihr/, as in *ear*.

ear	tear**	rear	Shakespeare
hear	dear	merely	cheerful
here	year	fear	superior
near	weary	interfere	beer

*There are many dialects of English that linguists call "r-less" because they do not have /r/ except *before vowels*. Such dialects are Southern British (Received Standard), parts of New York City, New England, and coastal Southern U. S. If your teacher speaks one of these dialects, you should imitate him, keeping in mind that his speech does not match the transcription given here.

** 'liquid from the eye', /tihr/.

Sentences

1. Keep the ear-phones nearer, dear.
2. Shakespeare's *King Lear* showed here last year.

2. The Sound /ehr/

Words frequently used

Practice the following common words containing the "long a-r sound"/ehr/, as in *air*.

air	their	fare	various
hair	there	fair	chair
care	where	Mary	spare
stairs	wear	tear (v.)	Claire

32

Sentences

3. Where are the stairs?
4. Careful! Don't tear it on that chair.

3. *The Sound* /ohr/

Words frequently used

Practice the following common words containing the "*o-r* sound" /ohr/, as in *four*.

1	2	3	4
four (4)	door	or	horse
fourteen (14)	floor	for	war
pour	store	fork	warm
more	pork	morning	short

Sentences

5. This store has four floors.
6. George just bought a four-door Ford.

NOTE: Many speakers have the vowel /oh/ in the words in all the columns 1, 2, 3, and 4. Some other speakers have that vowel in the words in Columns 1 and 2, and the "short *o* sound" /ɔ/ as in *boss*, in the words in Columns 3 and 4 and similar words. Such speakers have a contrast between *horse* and *hoarse*, *morning* and *mourning*, *war* and *wore*. Imitate your teacher's pronunciation.

There is considerable difference in pronunciation of these words in various parts of the United States. Some have /oh/ in Columns 1 and 2, and /ɔh/ in Columns 3 and 4; other speakers may have /oh/ in all these words, or /ɔh/ in all.

4. *The Sound* /uhr/

Words frequently used

Practice the following common words with the "long *u-r* sound"/uhr/, as in *sure*.

sure	you're	Moore	tour
cure	(welcome)	curious	tourist
pure	your	jury	insurance
poor			

Sentences

7. Tourists should be sure to drink pure water.
8. Be sure to check your life insurance.

NOTE: Many speakers pronounce *your*, *poor*, and other words spelled with *oo* and *u*, with the same vowel sound which you practiced in 3, on page 33, /ohr/. They are often the same speakers who use two different vowels in the words with /ohr/ in the words in Columns 1 and 2 like *store*, and /ɔhr/ in the words in Columns 3 and 4, like *horse*.

Imitate your teacher's pronunciation.

5. *The Sound* /a(h)r/

Words frequently used

Practice the following common words containing the "*a-r* sound" /ar, ahr/, as in *are*.

1	2	3	4
are	far	yard	tomorrow
R	heart	bar	sorry
March	hard	barred	orange
large	army	parking	Florida
car	par(don me)	farm	Oregon

A speaker from the New York City area says /ar/ or /ahr/ in all these words. Some speakers say /ar/ or /ɔr/ in the words in Column 4, like *sorry*. New England speech characteristically has /æ(h)r/ for /a(h)r/, as in *park the car*. Imitate your teacher's pronunciation.

Sentences

9. Park the car in the back yard.
10. Florida and Oregon are pretty far apart.

6. *The Sound* /ə(h)r/

Words frequently used

Practice the following common words containing the "*ur* sound"
/ər, əhr/, as in *were*.

were	learn	worse	skirt
thirteen	person	worst	shirt
thirty	sir	first	hurry
Thursday	girl	early	verb
her	nervous	work	thorough
worry	burn	world	earth

Sentences

11. Were the little girls with her, sir?
12. Learn the first thirty verbs thoroughly.

7. *Vowels Before R*

Words in contrast

The vowel sounds before *r* which you have studied in 1-6 of
Group VII are reviewed below. The contrasts are those made
in one variety of standard Northeastern speech. Remember that
there are many correct ways of pronouncing American English,
and that there are very many differences, from region to region,
in the pronunciation of the simple and complex vowels before
r.

Listen, then repeat: (First repeat each column 1, 2, etc.), then
repeat each line (1, 2, etc.).

1 /ihr/	2 /ehr/	3 /ohr/	4 /uhr/	5 /a(h)r/	6 /ə(h)r/
1. ear	air	oar	-----	are	err
2. peer	pair	pour	poor	par	purr
3. mere	mare	more	moor	mar	myrrh
4. sear	Sarah	sore	-----	Saar	sir
5. tear (n.)	tear (v.)	tore	tour	tar	turn

Sentences

13. The girls were wearing scarves and ear-
    muffs and their warmest coats.
14. We're parking your car over there.

Pronunciation Drill 14

8. *Sounds* /ər ihr/

Words in contrast

Now you will hear some pairs of words which differ in their
vowel sounds: the first word has the "*ur* sound" /ər, əhr/,
as in *were*; the second word has the "long *e-r* sound" /ihr/,
as in *ear*.

her	here	were	we're	bird	beard	fur	fear
worry	weary	purse	pierce	sir	seer	word	weird
purr	peer	err	ear	bur	beer	stir	steer
		myrrh	mere	shirr	sheer		

Sentences

15. We're always here on Thursday, sir.
16. Herbert's girl friend lives near here.
17. Is this your first year at Burlington University?

9. *Sounds* /ər ehr/

Words in contrast

Now you will hear some pairs of words which differ in their
vowel sounds: the first word has the "*ur* sound" /ər, əhr/,
as in *were*; the second word has the "long *a-r* sound" /ehr/,
as in *air*.

err	air	stir	stair	her	hair	whir	where
were	wear	stirred	stared	purr	pair	fur	fare
hurry	hairy	cur	care	bur	bear		

36

Sentences

18. We're wearing their shirts.
19. Is it thirty years since we were there?
20. Here's where we were working.

10. *Sounds* /ə(h)r a(h)r o(h)r/

Words in contrast

Now you will hear some pairs of words which differ only in their vowel sound: the first word has the "*ar* sound" /ar, ahr/, as in *are*; the second word has the "*ur* sound" /ər, əhr/, as in *were*.

are	err	far	fur	star	stir	hard	heard
heart	hurt	bard	bird	carve	curve		

Now you will hear some other pairs of words: the first word has the "*or* sound" /or, ohr/, as in *pore*; the second word has the "*ur* sound" /ər, əhr/, as in *were*.

pour	purr	sport	spurt	warm	worm	store	stir
hoard	heard	oar	err	for	fur	coarse	curse
born	burn	torn	turn	war	were		

Sentences

21. *Are* and *were* are parts of the verb *to be*.
22. Are the girls learning any more German?
23. George and Charles were warmly dressed.

11. *Vowels Before R*

Review

Review the sentences which you studied in PD 13 and 14.

A. Sentences with /ihr/

1. Keep the earphones nearer, dear.
2. Shakespeare's *King Lear* showed here last year.

B. Sentences with /ehr/

   3. Where are the stairs?
   4. Careful! Don't tear it on that chair.

C. Sentences with /o(h)r/

   5. This store has four floors.
   6. George just bought a four-door Ford.

D. Sentences with /uhr/

   7. Tourists should be sure to drink pure water.
   8. Be sure to check your life insurance.

E. Sentences with /a(h)r/

   9. Park the car in the back yard.
  10. Karl and Charles are pretty far apart.

F. Sentences with /ə(h)r/

  11. Were the little girls with her, sir?
  12. Learn the first 30 verbs thoroughly.

G. Sentences with /Vr/ in contrast

  13. The girls were wearing scarves and earmuffs and their warmest coats.
  14. We're parking your car over there.

H. Sentences with /ər ihr/

  15. We're always here on Thursday, sir.
  16. Herbert's girl friend lives near here.
  17. Is this your first year at the University?

I. Sentences with /ər ihr ehr/

  18. We're wearing their shirts.
  19. Is it thirty years since we were there?
  20. Here's where we were working.

J. Sentences with /ər o(h)r a(h)r/

  21. *Are* and *were* are parts of the verb *to be*.
  22. Are the girls learning any more German?
  23. George and Charles were warmly dressed.

Grammatical Endings, Stress, and Intonation

Pronunciation Drill 15

1. *Grammatical Endings*

English has very few grammatical suffixes. Adverbs, conjunctions, prepositions, and exclamations do not have grammatical suffixes. Some adjectives, but not all adjectives, have suffixes for comparison: *-er* /ər/ for the comparative degree, and *-est* /ɪst/ for the superlative degree, (rich, richer, richest; poor, poorer, poorest). Nouns and verbs may have grammatical endings, and pronouns have different forms and endings.

Pronouns. All pronouns have a subject form, an object form, and two possessive forms. *Listen, then repeat*:

Subject Form:	I	you	he	she	it	who	we	they
Object Form:	me	you	him	her	it	who(m)	us	them
1st *Possessive Form*: (before nouns)	my	your	his	her	its	whose	our	their
2nd *Possessive Form*: (not before nouns)	mine	yours	his	hers		whose	ours	theirs

Here are sentences which use all four forms of the pronouns.

1. I put my money on the table, and John asked me if it was mine.
2. You put your money on the table, and John asked you if it was yours.
3. She put her money on the table, and John asked her if it was hers.
4. We put our money on the table, and John asked us if it was ours.
5. They put their money on the table, and John asked them if it was theirs.

Nouns. Most nouns have a singular form, a plural form, a singular possessive form, and a plural possessive form.

Singular:	cat	dog	judge	wife	man
Plural:	cats	dogs	judges	wives	men
Singular Possessive:	cat's	dog's	judge's	wife's	man's
Plural Possessive:	cats'	dogs'	judges'	wives'	men's

The plural ending *s*, and the possessive endings *'s* and *s'* of the same noun are all pronounced alike. The *Noun Suffixes* (*s*, *'s*, and *s'*) are pronounced in one of three different ways /s, iz, z/ depending on the last sound of the noun.

For example, the *s* in *cats*, *cat's*, *cats'* is pronounced /s/;
the *s* in *dogs*, *dog's*, *dogs'* is pronounced /z/;
the *s* in *judges*, *judge's*, *judges'* is pronounced /iz/.

Noun Suffixes. The pronunciation of the noun suffixes (-*s*, -*'s*, -*s'*) is determined by the last sound of the noun. In column 1 below, the sounds followed by /s/ are listed, together with key words; in column 3 below, the sounds followed by /z/ are listed, together with key words; in column 2 below, the sounds followed by /iz/ are listed, together with key words.

Column 1 /s/	Column 2 /iz/
after P, PE, T, TE, K, KE, F, FE, PH, GH, TH, etc.	after S, SE, CE, Z, ZE, X, (T)CH, (D)GE
/p/ maps, tapes, stamps	/s/ uses (n.) places, taxes
/t/ seats, lights satellites	/z/ uses (v.) Liz's, quizzes
/k/ checks, headaches, snakes	/š/ ashes, wishes
	/ž/ garages
/f/ roofs, staff's photographs, coughs Ralph's	/č/ matches, Rich's, niches
	/j/ judges', edges

40

after vowel-spellings, and
B, BE, D, DE, G, GUE,
VE, THE, M, ME, N, NE,
NG, L, LE, R, RE

/V/	ties, Joe's	/m/	names, claims
/b/	clubs, Abe's	/n/	fans, Anne's
/d/	Ed's, cathodes	/ŋ/	songs, kings'
/g/	eggs, plagues	/l/	smiles, walls
/v/	wives', waves	/r/	car's, ears
/ð/	lathes, clothes		

Verbs.

The verb "to be" has these forms: *be, am, is, are, being, been, was, were.* All other verbs have a maximum of five different forms. (Tenses and moods are really phrases of 2 to 4 words, one of which words is one of the five different forms below.)

1. Common form:

| walk | sing | beat | lie | wish | knit |

2. 3rd singular form:

| walks | sings | beats | lies | wishes | knits |

3. Present participle form:

| walking | singing | beating | lying | wishing | knitting |

4. Past form:

| walked | sang | beat | lay | wished | knitted |

5. Past participle form:

| walked | sung | beaten | lain | wished | knitted |

Practice the pronunciation of the *Verb Suffix* for the 3rd singular form, used after *he, she, it* and singular *Nouns* and *Pronouns* (as in *he says , she has, it does, who is, the man sings*). The pronunciation of the *Verb Suffix (E)S* is identical with the pronunciation of the *Noun Suffixes* which you studied on Page 40. It is pronounced one of three different ways with /s, ɨz, z/ depending on the last sound of the common form of the verb.

For example, the *s* in *walks, beats, knits* is pronounced /s/;
the *s* in *sings, lies* is pronounced /z/;
the *es* in *wishes* is pronounced /ɨz/.

Verb Suffixes.

The pronunciation of the "third singular verb suffix", spelled *-s* or *es*, is always /s, z, ɨz/ added to the *Common Form* of the verb.

There are only four verbs in English which do not follow this rule.

I am - he is,   I do - he does,
I say - he says,   I have - he has

All the other regular verbs are in three classes: Column 1 has verbs with final sounds followed by /s/; Column 2 has verbs with final sounds followed by /ɨz/, and Column 3 has verbs with final sounds followed by /z/, all with key words. *Repeat the Key Words.*

Column 1		Column 2	
/s/		/ɨz/	
after P, PE, T, TE, K, KE, F, FE, PH, GH, TH, etc.		after S, SE, CE, Z, ZE, SH, X, (T)CH, (D)GE	
/p/	helps, stops, wipes	/s/	notices, increases, kisses
/t/	wants, fits, rotates	/z/	uses, oozes, buzzes
/k/	works, takes, checks	/š/	rushes, cashes
/f/	laughs, coughs, rebuffs	/č/	reaches, itches
/θ/	(rare)	/j/	changes, obliges

Column 3
/z/
after vowel-spellings
and B, BE, D, DE, G,
GUE, VE, THE, M, ME,
N, NE, NG, L, LE, R, RE

/V/	ties, knows, sees	/m/	seems, times
/b/	grabs	/n/	means, learns
/d/	attends, decides	/ŋ/	longs for, sings
/g/	drags, begs	/l/	smiles, calls
/v/	lives, arrives	/r/	hears, cares, remembers
/ð/	bathes, breathes		

Verbs Ending in -ED.

Many verbs called "regular verbs" have *-ed* as their past ending, or *-d* if the verb already has an *e* as its last letter. This ending is pronounced /t/ or /d/ *in the same syllable* with the verb, unless the last letters of the verb are *t, d, te,* or *de.*

As in *Verb Suffixes,* the regular verbs fall into three classes: Column 1 has verbs with final sounds followed by /ɨd/, Column 2 has verbs with final sounds followed by /t/, Column 3 has verbs with final sounds followed by /d/. *Say the Key Words:*

Column 1
/ɨd/
after T, TE, DE

| /t/ | wanted, fitted, seated, waited, expected, delighted, rested, rotated, completed |
| /d/ | needed, attended, added, crowded, decided, faded |

Column 2
/t/
after P, PE, (T)CH, K, KE, F, FE, PH, GH, TH, S, SE, X, SH

/p/	helped, stopped, wiped
/č/	reached, itched
/k/	checked, worked, asked, talked, smoked, baked
/f/	laughed, coughed, rebuffed
/θ/	frothed
/s/	noticed, increased, kissed, dressed, taxed
/s/	rushed, cashed

43

Column 3
/d/
after vowel-spellings and all other voiced consonants—
B, BE, (D)GE, G,
GUE, V, THE, M, ME, N,
NE, NG, L, LE, R, RE

/V/	tied, allowed	/n/	learned, cleaned
/b/	grabbed	/ŋ/	longed for
/j/	judged	/l/	smiled, called
/g/	dragged, begged	/r/	heard, cared, remembered
/v/	lived, arrived		
/ð/	bathed, breathed		

2. Stress

Stress Patterns.

Stress means "loudness". In English, there are four grades of stress. Often, a small difference in the stress pattern makes a large difference in the meaning.

Here are the names of the four grades of stress, and two ways to represent them:

Names of Stress	Dot Symbol	Accent Symbol
Weak (quiet)	•	˘
Tertiary (loud)	•	ˋ
Secondary (louder)	●	˄
Primary (loudest)	●	ˊ

Here is a well-known example of two different stress patterns on the same phrase:

 ● •
 1. White House
    The president lives in the White Hòuse.

 • ●
 2. white house
    The family lives in the whîte hoúse.

 ● •   ● ●
White Hoùse   whîte hoúse

Stress patterns on words.

Below are the five most frequent stress patterns. They consist of Primary Stresses and Weak Stresses. Notice the occurrence of the vowels /ə/ and /ɨ/ in weak syllables.

●	● •	• ●	● • •	• ● •
yés	áftĕr	bĕfóre	cómpănў	ănóthĕr
no	city	enough	possible	together
man	little	believe	usual	consider
good	saying	result	happily	tomorrow
fast	added	above	gathering	believing

Here are some other stress patterns consisting of one Primary
Stress and one or more Weak Stresses:

● ●..	● ●..	● ●... ●	● ...
Ămérĭcă	ĕxpérĭeňce	ĭmmédĭătelў	pássiŏnătelў
American	especially	imaginative	practicable
Republican	material	conditionally	amicable

Other stress patterns on words.

On Page 45, you practiced stress patterns consisting of Primary
and Weak Stresses. Many words have one Primary Stress, one
Tertiary Stress, and some Weak Stresses:

● ●	●..	●...	● ●.	● ●...
ráincòat	réălìze	éstĭmàtĕd	ăppréciate	ăppréciàtĕd
also	indicate	operator	intensify	intensifying
increase (n.)	satisfied	territory	intimidate	intimidated
blackbird	holiday	qualitative	infanticide	romanticizing
locate	telephone	telephoning		

● ●	● ●.	.. ●	.. ●.
ĭncréase (v.)	hòwévĕr	àftĕrnóon	ĭnfŏrmátiŏn
herself	already	understand	competition
themselves	whatever	represent	education
humane	re-doing	guarantee	operation
cartoon	unfeeling	disappoint	Democratic

● ..●..	. .●..
ànthrŏpŏlógĭcăl	pòssibĭlitў
sociometrical	satisfactory
regimentational	unconditional

●..● .	● ..●...
spècĭfĭcátiŏns	ànthrŏpŏlógĭcăllў
mathematician	sociometrically
semicoherent	

There are a few pairs of words in English which are alike except for the stress pattern. They have different meanings. Say the words below:

● ·　· ● · ●　　● ·　　· ●　　● ·

Aúgŭst - aŭgúst　ímpórt(v.) - ímpòrt (n.)　pèrmĭt(v.) - pérmĭt(n.)

Stress contrasts.

Now you will hear some pairs of words which differ in having one Primary Stress, or a Primary Stress and a Weak Stress.

pop poppy	might mighty	itch itchy	rock rocky
Bob Bobby	shade shady	edge edgy	bag baggy
leaf leafy	pith pithy	sis sissy	bush bushy
move movie	rose rosy	room roomy	rain rainy
tang tangy	Bill Billy	star starry	cough coffee
sit city	red ready	laid lady	hill hilly
doll dolly	pat patty	part party	putt putty
dot Dotty	boot booty	stone stony	wind windy
droop droopy	tab tabby	Tom Tommy	pen penny

Sentences

1. Chicago is called the Windy City.
2. Billy, your coffee is ready.

Stress patterns on phrases.

Some of the stress patterns which appear with phrases consist of Primary Stresses, Tertiary Stresses, and Weak Stresses. *Listen* to the phrases below, classified by their stress patterns, *then repeat*:

· ●	· ●	· ●
ă dáy	ăt hóme	tŏ dó
an egg	in time	to say
the men	to bed	to think

● ˘   ● ˘

dó ĭt   ísn'ť
tell 'im   couldn't
say it   didn't

˘ ●   ˘ ●   ˘ ●   ˘ ●

pùt ón   hòw múch   a loàf of breád   càll úp
take off   quite fast   a lot of money   bring up
get on   has seen   ice cream   He's here
get off   was done   old maid   It is

● ˘   ● ˘   ● ˘

Póst Òffice   cóffee brèak   tíe pìn
phone call   swimming pool   pie tin
shaving cream ball game   girl friend
White House   fish net   ice cream

Other stress patterns on phrases.

Many stress patterns on phrases include the Secondary Stress. Every phrase includes only one Primary Stress and may have Secondary, Tertiary, and Weak Stresses.

Secondary + Primary is the usual pattern for adjective + noun; verb + adverb; and, in short sentences, noun + verb.

Adjective + Noun   Verb + Adverb   Noun + Verb

● ●   ● ●   ● ●

bîg bóy   wâlk fást   Jôhn's góne.
beautiful woman sing well   Dick sings.
white cap   come now   Marian decided.
four paws   eat quickly   Cows moo.
black car   jump off   Dogs bark.
white dress   come to   Horses neigh.

48

Stress patterns in contrast.

The same phrase has one meaning if its stress pattern is Secondary   Primary (ˆ + ´), and a different meaning if its stress pattern includes a Tertiary Stress. *Listen* to the following phrases in contrast, *Then Repeat*:

Secondary+Primary	Primary+Tertiary	Tertiary+Primary
● ●	● •	• ●
ˆ ´	´ `	` ´

1. old maid
   (former servant)

                                   1a. old maid
   (spinster)

2. Paul Jones
   (a man's name)

                                   2a. Paul Jones
   (name of a dance)

3. red cap
   (hat which is red)

3a. redcap
   (porter)

4. blue bird
   (a bird which is blue)

4a. bluebird
   (certain species of bird)

5. black board
   (a piece of wood that is black)

5a. blackboard
   (writing surface in a classroom)

6. (four)-foot steps
   (steps which are 4 feet high)

6a. (four) footsteps
   (sound or impression of feet)

7. four paws
   (all 4 feet of an animal)

7a. forepaws
   (the 2 front feet of an animal)

8. long island
   (an island which is long)

                                   8a. Long Island
   (name of an island off New York)

9. white house
   (a house which is white)

9a. White House
   (President's house)

10. iced cream
   (cream which is iced)

10a. ice cream
   (dessert)

10b. ice cream
   (dessert)

Sentences

1. Is the White House really a white house?

2. Long Island really is a long island.

3. *Intonation*

Intonation is the tune of what we say, or the way our voices go up and down as we speak. In English there are four significant levels of pitch. Pitch means the highness or lowness of the voice. We can represent the four pitches in English in this way:

The lowest pitch (represented on line 1) is usually used at the end of sentences. A higher pitch (represented on line 2) is usually used at the beginning of sentences. In a long sentence, most of the words will be spoken on this pitch. A still higher pitch (represented on line 3) is also used. The strongest stress usually occurs with the highest pitch in a sentence, but this is not always true. The highest pitch of all (represented on line 4) is not used as often as the other three. It has a special connotation such as emphasis, surprise, or emotion.

The most frequent intonation pattern in English is the 2-3-1 pattern. That is, the sentence begins on pitch two, goes up to pitch three, and goes down to pitch one at the end. This rise or fall, to or toward another pitch, may occur in one syllable. We call this a glide. Glides usually occur with the strongest stress.

Below are some examples of sentences having the 2-3-1 intonation pattern.

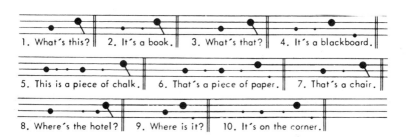

A variation of the 2-3-1 pattern is the 3-1 pattern. This is used in short sentences and phrases, usually when the strongest stress occurs on the first syllable. Below are some examples of phrases and sentences having the 3-1 pattern.

Yes.	Thank you.	Open it.
Please.	Close it.	Look at him.
No.	Tell me.	Give him some.
Thanks.	Hi, there.	Have a piece.
Fine.	Yes, sir.	Wait a while.

Practice counting, using the 3-1 intonation.

One. Two. Three. Four. Five. Six. Seven. Eight. Nine. Ten.

The 2-3-2 intonaton pattern is also frequently used in English. Below are some sentences and phrases with the 2-3-2 pattern.

1. Excuse me, please. 2. I'm fine, thank you. 3. Good-by. 4. So long.

5. Open the window, please. 6. Write it in your notebooks, please. 7. I study hard.

A variation of this pattern is the 3-2 pattern.

8. Fine, thanks. 9. Hi, Dick. 10. That's right. 11. O. K.

52

The 2-3. or rising intonation pattern is used in English, usually for a question that can be answered with yes or no. Below are some examples.

A rising intonation turns a statement into a question.

If you say  you are making a statement.

If you say you are asking a question.

Do NOT use the rising intonation with a statement construction unless you mean to ask a question.

Uses Of The Intonation Patterns.

Falling Intonation:

2-3-1   3-1   2-3-2

Statements:

2 It's 3 raining. 1   3 John's here. 1   2 I'm 3 fine, thanks. 2

Commands:

2 Close the 3 door. 1   3 Tell me. 1   2 Open the 3 window, please. 2

Questions Except Those To Be Answered By Yes or No

2 What 3 time is it? 1   3 Who's coming? 1   2 Who 3 is it? 2

Rising Intonation:
2-3

Questions Which Can Be Answered By Yes Or No

2 Is it time for 3 dinner? 3   2 Do you have a 3 pencil? 3
2 Can you speak 3 English? 3

Questions Constructed Like A Statement

2 She went to 3 school today? 3   2 This bus goes to 3 town? 3
2 You went to the 3 movies? 3

Review

Below are some questions with the 2-3-1 intonation pattern.

1. What do they cost?   2. Who are Sarah and Fred?   3. When do you want to move?

4. How does the machine work?   5. Well, what kind of cigarettes do you want?

6. How much do I owe you? ‖ 7. Where is your wife | now? ‖

8. What time does the lecture start? ‖ 9. Where do you want us to meet you? ‖

10. And what do you want to drink: ‖ coffee, | tea, | or milk? ‖

Below are some statements with the 2-3-1 intonation pattern.

1. I'm going to the movies this evening. ‖ 2. The class begins | at nine o'clock. ‖

3. Your living room | is very attractive. ‖ 4. Our home | is on the other side of the city. ‖

5. This is a single room | with a private bath. ‖ 6. I have two tickets to the baseball

game | next Saturday. ‖ 7. I can use the telephone | in that drugstore | over there. ‖

8. There's a dance | at the International Student House | Friday night. ‖

9. I'd like some orange juice, | two eggs, | bacon, | and toast. ‖

10. He wants to find | an American roommate | so he can practice his English. ‖

PART II

CONSONANTS

GROUP IX

Consonants /θ ð s z t d/

Pronunciation Drill 18

1. *Consonants /θ ð/*

Words frequently used

In English, the letters *th* represent two different sounds: the "voiced *th* sound" as in *they*, and the "voiceless *th* sound", as in *think*. Both sounds are made by putting the tongue between the teeth, but the sound written /θ/ is voiceless, like /f/, and the sound written /ð/ is voiced, like /v/.

The "voiced *th* sound" is the first sound in a very small number of English words (around twenty), but many of these words are used with very great frequency. The common words are given in the first three columns (1, 2, 3) below. Words in the fourth column (4) are archaic or rare.

Practice the following common words with the "voiced *th* sound" /ð/, as in *they*.

1	2	3	4
the	they	then	thou
this	them	than	thee
that	their	thus	thy
these	theirs	though	thine
those	there	therefore	thither, thence

The voiced *th* sound is also found in the middle of words, and at the end of words where it is regularly spelled *-the* (Exceptions: *smooth*, and sometimes *with*.)

mother	another	northern	either
father	rather	southern	neither
brother	bother	smoother	bather
weather	whether	smooth(e)	bathe

58

Sentences

1. My brothers did that themselves.
2. Their car is better than this one.
3. Are they going there some other day, Mother?
4. Although these southern cities have better weather,
   I'd rather visit the northern ones.

2. *The Consonant* /θ/

Words frequently used

Practice the following common words containing the "voiceless *th* sound" /θ/, as in *think*.

think	thirteen	month	theater
thought	thirty	mouth	anything
thanks	third	south	everything
thorough	thousand	healthy	nothing
thumb	thing	wealthy	mathematical

The voiceless *th* sound is the last sound in a number of nouns.

warm - warmth (noun)	long - length (n.)
heal - health (n.)	breathe - breath (n.)
strong - strength (n.)	wide - width (n.)
deep - depth (n.)	

The suffix -*th* is used to make the adjective forms of the numbers, beginning with 4.

fourth fifth sixth seventh eighth ninth tenth eleventh twelfth thirteenth fourteenth fifteenth twentieth fiftieth hundredth thousandth.

Sentences

5. Let's thank her for the theater tickets.
6. *Thick* and *thin* mean opposite things.
7. Does the month of June have thirty days, or thirty-one?
8. I thought I'd go south, not north.

3. Consonants /θð/

Now you will hear some pairs of words which differ in having the "voiceless *th* sound" /θ/, as in *think*, or the "voiced *th* sound" /ð/, as in *they*. The first word has /θ/; the second word has /ð/.

thigh - thy	teeth - teethe
wrath - rather	wreath - wreathe
mouth - mouthe	lath - lather
sooth - soothe	ether - either
zither - dither	sheath - sheathing

Sentences

9. This is the third toothbrush I've lost this month.
10. The baby's teething, so her mouth is rather sore.
11. Congratulations! You're the thousandth person to visit this theater.
12. Would you rather have gas or ether?
13. Neither gas nor ether—no anesthetics, thanks.
14. They have to think this thing through.

4. Consonants /θð/

Review Sentences

Review the sentences you practiced in PD 18.

A. Sentences with /ð/

1. My brothers did that themselves.
2. Their car is better than this one.
3. Are they going there some other day, Mother?
4. Although these southern cities have better weather, I'd rather visit the northern ones.

B. Sentences with /θ/

    5. Let's thank her for the theater tickets.
    6. *Thick* and *thin* mean opposite things.
    7. Does the month of June have thirty days, or thirty-one?
    8. I thought I'd go south, not north.

C. Sentences with /θ/ and /ð/

    9. This is the third toothbrush I've lost this month.
  10. The baby's teething, so her mouth is rather sore.
  11. Congratulations! You're the thousandth person to visit this theater.
  12. Would you rather have gas or ether?
  13. Neither gas nor ether—no anesthetics, thanks.
  14. They have to think this thing through.

Pronunciation Drill 19

5. Consonants /s z t d/

Words frequently used

In English, the "*s* sound" and the "*z* sound" are made by touching the sides of the tongue to the tooth ridge, and letting a stream of air come out over the middle of the tongue, which is curved. The opening at the middle of the tongue is small. The "*s* sound" is voiceless, like /f/, and the "*z* sound" is voiced like /v/.

Practice the following common words containing the "*s* sound" /s/, as in *say*.

say	sister	S	this
see	Mr. (Mister)	Miss	us
C	professor	nice	listen
6, 16, 60	person	place	use (n.)
7, 17, 70	possible	worse	less

61

Sentences

1. *See* and *say* begin with *s*.
2. Miss Ross said yes.
3. Did your sister send this to us?
4. Is Sunday the second of September?

6. *The Consonant* /z/

Words frequently used

Practice the following common words containing the "*z* sound" /z/, as in *zero*.

zero	Tuesday	crazy	was	easy
Z	Wednesday	Missouri	is	business
zoo	Thursday	dessert	has	as
thousand	busy	his	does	says

Sentences

5. Please excuse me.
6. He always goes to the zoo on Thursdays.
7. Is his home in Arizona?
8. A thousand has three zeros.

7. *Consonants* /s z/

Words in contrast

Now you will hear some pairs of words which differ in having the "*s* sound" /s/, as in *sink*, or the "*z* sound" /z/, as in *zinc*. The first word has /s/; the second word has /z/.

sue	zoo	see	Z	sip	zip	ice	eyes
bus	buzz	hiss	his	niece	knees	piece	peas
cease	sees	decrease	decrees	close	close	scion	Zion
dice	dies	price	prize	loose	lose	face	phase
sink	zinc						

Sentences

9. She goes to the zoo to see the animals.
10. Sara's your sister, isn't she?
11. His suit is the same as this one.
12. What size dress does Susie wear?

8. *Consonants* /t d/

Words frequently used

In English, the "*t* sound" and the "*d* sound" are made by the tip of the tongue touching the ridge just above and behind the upper teeth. The tongue does not touch the teeth. The "*t* sound" is voiceless like /f/, and the "*d* sound" is voiced like /v/.

Practice the following common words containing the "*t* sound" /t/, as in *tell* , *little*, *button*.

1	2	3	4
tell	not	little	button
T	get	better	mountain
to, too, two	cigarette	butter	bitten
12, 10	wet	later	written
talk	sit	eating	satin
tall	let	sitting	gotten

In the middle of a word (see Column 3) *t* sounds like *d* in the speech of many Americans. *Listen, then repeat*: little, butter, better, put it away, latter, eating, eighty, later, bottom.

Before /n/ in a weak syllable (see Column 4), *t* has still another sound. The tongue is held at the tooth ridge. *Listen, then repeat*: button, mountain, fountain, kitten, bitten, written, rotten, satin.

The suffix *-ed* after certain sounds is pronounced like /t/. *Listen, then repeat*: helped, stooped, packed, laughed, promised, missed.

Sentences

13. Try to talk in English all the time.
14. Can you tell me the time?
15. You'd better put a little butter on it.
16. Is a better bottle of wine pretty expensive?
17. It was written by Mr. Sutton.
18. Don't button the bottom button of your jacket.

9. *The Consonant* /d/

Words frequently used

Remember that in English, the "*d* sound" is made by the tip of the tongue touching the ridge just above and behind the upper teeth. The tongue does not touch the teeth. The "*d* sound" is voiced like /v/.

Practice the following common words containing the "*d* sound" /d/, as in *day*.

day	don't	good	hold
D	dollar	bad	old
do	doing	could	hand
did	didn't	would	mind
done	idea	should	need
doctor	anybody	had	road
December	condition	find	hard

The suffix -*ed* after certain sounds is pronounced /d/. *Listen, then repeat*: lived, agreed, bathed, pulled, remembered·

Sentences

19. A *good* doctor wouldn't do that.
20. What day in December did he come?
21. I couldn't find the dollar I had.
22. Ted had a good idea, didn't he?

10. *Consonants* /t d s z θ ð/

Words in contrast

Now you will hear some pairs of words which differ in having the "*t* sound" /t/, as in *ten*, or the "*d* sound" /d/, as in *den*. The first word has /t/; the second word has /d/.

tin	din	tie	die	two	do	tee	D
tip	dip	town	down	tome	dome	time	dime
tell	dell	wait	wade	latter	ladder	bitter	bidder
matter	madder	satin	sadden	written	ridden	height	hide
bet	bed	wrote	rode	bit	bid	late	laid
rot	rod	mate	maid	plate	played	light	lied

Sentences

23. Tell Dotty to do it.
24. Today is cold, isn't it?
25. Ted said he couldn't stay for dessert.
26. Don't you know the word *date*?

11. *Consonants* /t θ s/

Words in contrast

Now you will hear some groups of words which differ in having the "*t* sound" /t/, as in *tin*, the "*th* sound" /θ/, as in *thin*, or the "*s* sound" /s/, as in *sin*. The first word has /t/, the second word has /θ/, and the third word has /s/.

tin	thin	sin	taught	thought	sought	tank	thank	sank
tick	thick	sick	tinker	thinker	sinker	true	threw	sue
taw	thaw	saw	teem	theme	seem			

27. Thanks for the cigarettes, Miss Thorp.
28. Sixteen times two equals thirty-two.
29. The best theater tickets cost from three to six dollars.
30. Thursday and Sunday were hot, but today is nice.

12. *Consonants* /d ð z/

Words in contrast

Now you will hear some groups of words which differ in having the "*d* sound" /d/, as in *den*, the "voiced *th* sound" /ð/, as in *then*, and the "*z* sound" /z/, as in *Zen*. The first word has /d/, the second word has /ð/, and the third word has /z/.

den	then	Zen	dine	thine	resign
breeding	breathing	breezing	ladder	lather	lazar
teed	teethe	tease	bayed	bathe	baize
D	thee	Z	lied	lithe	lies
seed	seethe	seize			

Sentences

31. Their ideas are always good.
32. They have Wednesday off, don't they?
33. These old roads are in bad condition.
34. Is his father a doctor?

13. *Consonants* /s z t d θ ð/

Review Sentences

Review the sentences you practiced in PD 19 and 20.

A. Sentences with /s/

1. *See* and *say* begin with s.
2. Miss Ross said yes.
3. Did your sister send this to us?
4. Is Sunday the second of September?

B. Sentences with /z/

    5. Please excuse me.
    6. He always goes to the zoo on Thursdays.
    7. Is his home in Arizona?
    8. A thousand has three zeros.

C. Sentences with /s/ and /z/

    9. She goes to the zoo to see the animals.
  10. Sara's your sister, isn't she?
  11. His suit is the same as this one.
  12. What size dress does Susie wear?

D. Sentences with /t/

  13. Try to talk in English all the time.
  14. Can you tell me the time?
  15. You'd better put a little butter on it.
  16. Is a better bottle of wine pretty expensive?
  17. It was written by Mr. Sutton.
  18. Don't button the bottom button of your jacket.

E. Sentences with /d/

  19. A *good* doctor wouldn't do that.
  20. What day in December did he come?
  21. I couldn't find the dollar I had.
  22. Ted had a good idea, didn't he?

F. Sentences with /t/ and /d/

  23. Tell Dotty to do it.
  24. Today is cold, isn't it?
  25. Ted said he couldn't stay for dessert.
  26. Don't you know the word *date*?

G. Sentences with /t/, /θ/, and /s/

27. Thanks for the cigarettes, Miss Thorp.
28. Sixteen times two equals thirty-two.
29. The best theater tickets cost from three
    to six dollars.
30. Thursday and Sunday were hot, but today
    is nice.

H. Sentences with /d/, /ð/, and /z/

31. Their ideas are always good.
32. They have Wednesday off, don't they?
33. These old roads are in bad condition.
34. Is his father a doctor?

GROUP X

Consonants /f v w h y j č š/

Pronunciation Drill 21

1. *Consonants* /f v w/

Words frequently used

In English, the "*f* sound" is made by touching the upper teeth to the lower lip, and letting the breath come out between them. The sounds /f/ and /v/ are alike, except that the "*f* sound" is voiceless, like /t/.

Practice the following common words containing the "*f* sound" /f/, as in *fine*.

fine	four	coffee	life
for	five	different	off
first	fourteen	awful	if
find	fifteen	information	laugh
family	forty	telephone	leaf

Sentences

1. They went to the cafeteria for some coffee.
2. California has a fine climate.
3. This room has comfortable furniture.
4. If you don't know the telephone number, call information.

2. *The Consonant* /v/

Words frequently used

The "*v* sound" is made by the upper teeth touching the lower lip.

Practice the following common words containing the "v sound" /v/, as in *very*.

very	visit	November	live
V	vegetable	of	five
verb	seven	over	move
vowel	eleven	ever	have
vacant	seventeen	every	leave
vacation	seventy	never	believe
value	evening	several	twelve

Sentences

5. I live very near Avery Avenue.
6. All English vowels are voiced.
7. Have you ever visited Vicksburg?
8. Five and seven make twelve.   (5 + 7 = 12)

3. Consonants /f v/

Words in contrast

Now you will hear some pairs of words which differ only in having the "*f* sound" /f/, as in *fine*, or the "*v* sound"/v/, as in *vine*. Remember that the position of the lips and teeth is the same for these two sounds. The only difference is that /f/ is voiceless, like /t/, and /v/ is voiced, like /d/. In the pairs below, the first word has /f/, and the second word has /v/.

fine	vine	life	live	leaf	leave	fan	van
belief	believe	file	vile	fee	V	few	view
feel	veal	fat	vat	half	halve	shuffle	shovel
raffle	ravel	feign	vane	fear	veer	foil	voile

Sentences

9. During the first fall days, the leaves
   turn lovely colors.
10. Do you find the English verbs very difficult?
11. I believe President Roosevelt died in 1945.
12. I'd like to move to the boarding house, if
    there's a comfortable room vacant.

70

4. The Consonant /w/

Words frequently used

The "*w* sound" in English is made with the lips rounded, and the tongue high and back, at the beginning of the sound. The sound is voiced, like /d/.

Practice the following common words containing the "*w* sound" /w/, as in *week*.

week	wait	won't	were
one	work	wonder	was
well	wish	welcome	willing
woman	will	window	weather
women	with	anyway	weight
want	would	warm	world

Note: Several common English words spelled with *wh* are pronounced by some Americans with the /hw/ sound, and by others with the /w/ sound. Either is correct. Imitate your teacher and the other educated speakers around you. The most common words in this category are: where, why, when, what, and which.

Sentences

13. We always walk to work.
14. One day a week, we usually wash our clothes.
15. Why do you want to know?
16. The weather was warm this week, wasn't it?

5. Consonants /w v/

Words in contrast

Now you will hear some pairs of words which differ in having the "*w* sound" /w/, as in *wine*, or the "*v* sound" /v/, as in *vine*. The first word has /w/; the second word has /v/.

wet	vet	wow	vow	we	v	wine	vine
wane	vane	wiper	viper	Willa	villa	wail	veil
went	vent	west	vest	wick	Vic		

17. Why can't Washingtonians ever vote?
18. When our friends leave, we wave good-bye to them.
19. Are Nevada and Wyoming western states?
20. I believe Virginia and West Virginia are very near Washington.

6. *Consonants* /f v w/

Review sentences

Review the sentences you practiced in PD 21.

A. Sentences with /f/

1. They went to the cafeteria for some coffee.
2. California has a fine climate.
3. This room has comfortable furniture.
4. If you don't know the telephone number, call information.

B. Sentences with /v/

5. I live very near Avery Avenue.
6. All English vowels are voiced.
7. Have you ever visited Vicksburg?
8. Five and seven make twelve.

C. Sentences with /f/ and /v/

9. During the first fall days, the leaves turn lovely colors.
10. Do you find English verbs very difficult?
11. I believe President Roosevelt died in 1945.
12. I'd like to move to the boarding house, if there's a comfortable room vacant.

D. Sentences with /w/

13. We always walk to work.
14. One day a week, we usually wash our clothes.
15. Why do you want to know?
16. The weather was warm this week, wasn't it?

E. Sentences with /w/ and /v/

17. Why can't Washingtonians ever vote?
18. When our friends leave, we wave good-bye to them.
19. Are Nevada and Wyoming western states?
20. I believe Virginia and West Virginia are very near Washington.

Pronunciation Drill 22

7. *The Consonant* /h/

Words frequently used

The "*h* sound" in English is made by blowing the breath out. The lips and tongue are in the position for the following sound.

Practice the following common words containing the "*h* sound" /h/, as in *here*.

here	hundred	house	hand
hear	home	head	habit
how	ahead	heavy	half
hello	help	heard	hair
high	hard	hot	heat
who	hope	horse	health
whose	hotel	heart	human

Sentences

1. Here's your hat.
2. He likes hot dogs and hamburgers.
3. Is that a boarding house or a hotel?
4. How hot it is in here!

8. *The Consonant* /h/

Words in contrast

Now you will hear some pairs of words which differ in having,
or not having, the "*h* sound" /h/, as in *here*. The first word
does not have /h/; the second word has /h/.

ill	hill	am	ham	all	hall	air	hair
eat	heat	it	hit	at	hat	E	he
ear	hear	is	his	eye	hi	as	has
add	had	Ed	head	art	heart	and	hand
A	hay	ate	hate	odd	hod	old	hold
all	hall	owl	howl	arm	harm	ale	hale

Sentences

5. Is it *his* hat?
6. We hear with our ears.
7. Hello, Ellen.
8. I hate ham, but I ate it anyway.

9. *The Consonant* /y/

Words frequently used

At the beginning of the "*y* sound" the tongue
is in a high position toward the front of the
mouth. The middle of the tongue is near the
hard palate. The tip of the tongue does *not*
touch the ridge just behind the teeth.

Practice the following common words containing the "*y* sound"
/y/, as in *you*.

you	year	yes	billion
your	usually	yesterday	young
January	use (v.)	yet	beyond
excuse	use (n.)	yellow	yard
United States	few	million	Yankee

Sentences

9. Do you practice your English in class?
10. Is your sister younger than you?
11. Yale is a famous university in the United States.
12. Last year, they used to play tennis every day.

10. *The Consonant* /j/

Words frequently used

During the first part of the "*j* sound", the tip of the tongue touches the ridge just behind the upper teeth. The lips are pushed out a little. The "*j* sound" is voiced, like /d/.

Practice the following common words containing the "*j* sound" /j/, as in *job*.

job	joke	vegetable	large
G, J	Jack	subject	marriage
January	James	religion	George
June	jazz	engine	judge
July	germ	soldier	package
just	general	Georgia	language

Sentences

13. June, July, and January begin with *j*.
14. We have orange juice, grapefruit juice, and pineapple juice.
15. Did Jack and Joe just come?
16. George got a job selling vegetables.

11. *Consonants* /y j/

Words in contrast

Now you will hear some pairs of words which differ in having the "*y* sound" /y/, as in *yet*, or the "*j* sound" /j/, as in *jet*. The first word has /y/; the second word has /j/.

yam jam	yet jet	use juice	yellow jello
yell jell	yoke joke	yak Jack	you Jew
year jeer	Yale jail	yard jarred	yacht jot
ye G	use Jews	yea Jay	yon John

17. Lemon jello is yellow.
18. Have you flown in a jet plane yet?
19. Jack and George go to Yale University.
20. I like yams with ham, but not jam with ham.

12. *Consonants* /h y j/

Review sentences

Review the sentences you practiced in PD 22.

A. Sentences with /h/

1. Here's your hat.
2. He likes hot dogs and hamburgers.
3. Is that a boarding house or a hotel?
4. How hot it is in here!

B. Sentences with /h/ in contrast with initial vowel sound

5. Is it *his* hat?
6. We hear with our ears.
7. Hello, Ellen.
8. I hate ham, but I ate it anyway.

C. Sentences with /y/

9. Do you practice your English in class?
10. Is your sister younger than you?
11. Yale is a famous university in the United States.
12. Last year, they used to play tennis every day.

D. Sentences with /j/

13. June, July, and January begin with *j*.
14. We have orange juice, grapefruit juice, and pineapple juice.
15. Did Jack and Joe just come?
16. George got a job selling vegetables.

E. Sentences with /y/ and /j/

   17. Lemon jello is yellow.
   18. Have you flown in a jet plane yet?
   19. Jack and George go to Yale University.
   20. I like yams with ham, but not jam with ham.

Pronunciation Drill 23

13. *Consonants* /č š j/

Words frequently used

The "*ch* sound" in English is made with the tongue close to the palate, and the lips pushed out a little. The tip of the tongue touches the ridge just behind the upper teeth during the first part of the sound. The /č/ is voiceless like /t/, but otherwise it is like /j/.

Practice the following comon words containing the "*ch* sound" /č/, as in *child*.

child	check	teacher	much
children	chair	lecture	watch
chicken	cheap	furniture	teach
cheese	chin	actual	such
change	choose	luncheon	H

Sentences

1. The child was born in March.
2. Do you want a cheese sandwich or a chicken sandwich?
3. Which lecture did the teacher go to?
4. Don't choose a cheap watch.

14. *The Consonant* /š/

Words frequently used

The "*sh* sound" in English is made with the tip of the tongue close to the ridge behind the upper teeth, but *not* touching it. The tongue is curved; that is, the sides are higher than the middle. The lips are pushed out a little. The /š/ is voiceless, like /t/.

Practice the following common words containing the "*sh* sound" /š/, as in *she*.

she	short	direction	wish
shall	show	instructions	wash
should	shouldn't	special	cash
shoe	Chicago	examination	cashier
sure	shower	nation	shave
sugar	shop	national	shine

Sentences

5. She has some new dishes.
6. The instructions should show you how to use the machine.
7. Shall we wash our clothes, or brush them?
8. I wish my shoes were shined!

15. *Consonants* /č š/

Words in contrast

Now you will hear some pairs of words which differ in having the "*sh* sound' /š/, as in *ship*, or the "*ch* sound" /č/ as in *chip*. The first word has /š/; the second word has /č/.

ship	chip	shoe	chew	mush	much	marsh	march
dish	ditch	shop	chop	sheep	cheap	shoes	choose
wish	witch	cash	catch	washing	watching	mash	match
share	chair	she's	cheese	shin	chin		

Sentences

  9. Are you sure she has two children?
10. Where can I cash a check?
11. He's going to shave and take a shower before lunch.
12. We're watching conditions in Washington.

16. *Consonants* /č j/

Words in contrast
Remember that the /č/ and /j/ are alike, except that /č/ is voiceless like /t/, and /j/ is voiced like /d/.

Now you will hear some pairs of words which differ in having the "*ch* sound" /č/, as in *chin*, or the "*j* sound" /j/, as in *gin*.

chin	gin	cheep	jeep	etching	edging
larch	large	chew	Jew	chest	jest
match	Madge	Chet	jet	batch	badge
				choke	joke

Sentences

13. The children had vegetables and fruit juice for lunch.
14. George bought that chair last July.
15. Which subject does Mr. Jackson teach?
16. Did Charles and Joe enjoy the lecture?

17. *Consonants* /č š j/

Review sentences

Review the sentences you practiced in PD 23.

A. Sentences with /č/
  1. The child was born in March.
  2. Do you want a cheese sandwich, or a chicken sandwich?
  3. Which lecture did the teacher go to?
  4. Don't choose a cheap watch.

B. Sentences with /š/

   5. She has some new dishes.
   6. The instructions should show you how to use the machine.
   7. Shall we wash our clothes, or brush them?
   8. I wish my shoes were shined!

C. Sentences with /š/ and /č/

   9. Are you sure she has two children?
  10. Where can I cash a check?
  11. He's going to shave and take a shower before lunch.
  12. We're watching conditions in Washington.

D. Sentences with /č/ and /j/

  13. The children had vegetables and fruit juice for lunch.
  14. George bought that chair last July.
  15. Which subject does Mr. Jackson teach?
  16. Did Charles and Joe enjoy the lecture?

GROUP XI

Pronunciation Drill 24

1. *Consonants* /p b v/

Words frequently used

In English, the "*p* sound" and the "*b* sound" are both made by closing the lips and then opening them. The "*p* sound" is voiceless, like /t/, and the "*b* sound" is voiced, like /d/.

Practice the following common words containing the "*p* sound" /p/, as in *person*.

person	piece	people	keep
put	pie	couple	hope
P	pound	happen	up
pay	pack	simple	cup
possibly	suppose	open	map

Sentences

1. Please pay the cashier.
2. I'd like a piece of apple pie and a cup of coffee, please.
3. Paul, did you put the paper on the desk?
4. Don't push other people.

2. *Consonant* /b/

Words frequently used

Practice the following common words containing the "*b* sound" /b/, as in *be*.

be	Bob	bus	November
B	job	busy	December
big	baby	billion	cab
Boston	back	bad	best
about	but	good-bye	believe
possible	by	October	probably

Sentences

5. *Better* and *best* begin with B.
6. Bob's from Boston, I believe.
7. Isn't this new building beautiful?

3. *Consonants* /p b/

Words in contrast

Now you will hear some pairs of words which differ in having
the "*p* sound" /p/, as in *pea*, or the "*b* sound" /b/, as in *be*.
The first word has /p/; the second word has /b/.

pay	bay	pin	bin	maple	Mabel	sopping	sobbing
nip	nib	mop	mob	napped	nabbed	putt	but
pie	by	pound	bound	pack	back	cup	cub
Pete	beet	pet	bet				

Sentences

9. The program will probably begin about eight o'clock.
10. Pears and bananas are both fruits, but potatoes are
    vegetables.
11. Paul, you'd better buy this paper.
12. Which bus goes to the Capitol?

4. *Consonants* /b v/

Words in contrast

Remember that the "*b* sound" is made by closing the lips and
then opening them, and that the "*v* sound" is made by the
upper teeth touching the lower lip.

Now you will hear some pairs of words which differ in having
the "*b* sound" /b/, as in *bat*, or the "*v* sound" /v/, as in *vat*.
The first word has /b/; the second word has /v/.

bat vat	Boyd void	by vie	bet vet
Lib live	bane vane	boat vote	bale veil
boil voile	bend vend	saber saver	robe rove
cabs calves	lobes loaves	berry very	

Sentences

13. Bill is very much better today.
14. Every boy in school plays volley ball.
15. Do these berries grow on vines or bushes?
16. In English, *B* and *V* are both voiced.

5. *Consonants* /p b v/

Review Sentences

Review the sentences you practiced in PD 24.

A. Sentences with /p/

1. Please pay the cashier.
2. I'd like a piece of apple pie and a cup of coffee, please.
3. Paul, did you put the paper on the desk?
4. Don't push other people.

B. Sentences with /b/

5. *Better* and *best* begin with B.
6. Bob's from Boston, I believe.
7. Will you be back by October?
8. Isn't this new building beautiful?

C. Sentences with /p/ and /b/

9. The program will probably begin about eight o'clock.
10. Pears and bananas are both fruits, but potatoes are vegetables.
11. Paul, you'd better buy this paper.
12. Which bus goes to the Capitol?

D. Sentences with /b/ and /v/

13. Bill is very much better today.
14. Every boy in school plays volley ball.
15. Do these berries grow on vines or bushes?
16. In English, *B* and *V* are both voiced.

6. *Consonants* /k g p t č b d j/

Words frequently used

In English, the "*k* sound" and the "*g* sound" are made by touching the back part of the tongue to the soft palate. The "*k* sound" is voiceless, like /t/, and the "*g* sound" is voiced, like /d/.

Practice the following common words containing the "*k* sound" /k/, as in *come*.

come	back	car	check
welcome	key	coffee	breakfast
talk	instruction	look	came
call	American	book	cat
take	buckle	like	cake
make	luck	can	steak

Sentences
1. Most Americans have coffee for breakfast.
2. Where can I cash a check?
3. Call me at six o'clock.
4. Is he looking for work in a factory?

7. *The Consonant* /g/

Words frequently used

Practice the following common words containing the "*g* sound" /g/, as in *get*.

get	forget	girl	sugar
give	again	go	cigarette
guess	begin	garden	magazine
game	egg	good	dog
guest	big	August	dialogue

84

Sentences

5. The girl got eggs, cigarettes, and sugar.
6. Don't forget to study the dialogue.
7. Are you going to begin your vacation in August?
8. Is the weather good for your garden?

8. *Consonants* /k g/

Words in contrast

Now you will hear some pairs of words which differ in having the "*k* sound" /k/, as in *come*, or the "*g* sound" /g/, as in *gum*. The first word has /k/; the second word has /g/.

come gum	Kay gay	pick pig	muck mug
cull gull	Kate gate	plucked plugged	bicker bigger
call gall	could good	curl girl	duck dug
cane gain	luck lug	lacking lagging	leak league

Sentences

9. He always gets eggs and coffee for breakfast.
10. Call me again some time.
11. Did they get Lucky Strike cigarettes?
12. I've got to go to the bank to cash a check.

9. *Consonants* /p t č k/

Words frequently used

Practice the following common words containing the "*p* sound" /p/, as in *possible*, the "*ch* sound" /č/, as in *child*, the "*t* sound" /t/, as in *time*, or the "*k* sound" /k/, as in *car*. All these sounds are called "voiceless stops".

1	2	3	4
possible	time	child	car
put	table	cheese	call
open	little	teacher	because
happy	button	lecture	talking
cup	let	much	take
map	not	watch	mark

Sentences

13. I'd like a cup of coffee, and a piece of apple pie.
14. Can you tell me the time?
15. Which lecture did the teacher go to?
16. Where can I cash a check?

10. *Consonants* /b d j g/

Words frequently used

Practice the following common words containing the "*b* sound" /b/, as in *big*, the "*d* sound" /d/. as in *do*, the "*j* sound" /j/, as in *June*, and the "*g* sound" /g/, as in *get*. All these sounds are called "voiced stops".

1	2	3	4
big	do	June	get
believe	day	job	give
about	ready	vegetable	ago
table	reading	subject	together
job	good	large	bag
cab	bad	marriage	leg

Sentences

17. Bob's from Boston, I believe.
18. Ted had a good idea, didn't he?
19. George got a job selling vegetables.
20. Are you going to begin your vacation in August?

11. *Consonants* /k g p t č b d j/

Review sentences

Review the sentences you practiced in PD 25.

A. Sentences with /k/

1. Most Americans have coffee for
   breakfast.
2. Where can I cash a check?
3. Call me at six o'clock.
4. Is he looking for work in a factory?

B. Sentences with /g/

  5. The girl got eggs, cigarettes, and
     sugar.
  6. Don't forget to study the dialogue.
  7. Are you going to begin your vacation
     in August?
  8. Is the weather good for your garden?

C. Sentences with /k/ and /g/

  9. He always gets eggs and coffee for
     breakfast.
 10. Call me again some time.
 11. Did they get Lucky Strike cigarettes?
 12. I've got to go to the bank to cash a
     check

D. Sentences with /p/, /t/, /č/, or /k/

 13. I'd like a cup of coffee, and a piece
     of apple pie.
 14. Can you tell me the time?
 15. Which lecture did the teacher go to?
 16. Where can I cash a check?

E. Sentences with /b/, /d/, /j/, or /g/

 17. Bob's from Boston, I believe.
 18. Ted had a good idea, didn't he?
 19. George got a job selling vegetables.
 20. Are you going to begin your vacation
     in August?

Pronunciation Drill 26

12. *The Consonant* /ž/

Words frequently used

The "*zh* sound" in English is made with the tip of the tongue
close to the ridge just behind the upper teeth, but not touching
it. The tongue is curved; that is, the sides are higher than the
middle. The lips are often pushed out a little. The "*zh* sound"
is voiced, like /d/. This sound occurs in the middle and at
the end of English words, but not at the beginning.

Practice the following common words containing the "zh sound" /ž/, as in *measure*.

measure	division	collision	garage
vision	confusion	decision	beige
pleasure	conclusion	leisure	rouge

Sentences

1. I have to measure the garage.
2. The collision occurred because of the driver's poor vision.

13. *Consonants* /š ž/

Words in contrast

Now you wll hear some pairs of words which differ in having the "sh sound" /š/, as in *Aleutian*, or the "zh sound" /ž/, as in *allusion*. Remember that the mouth position is the same for these sounds, but /š/ is voiceless, like /t/, and /ž/ is voiced, like /d/.

ruche	rouge	Asher	azure
Aleutian	allusion	dilution	delusion
mesher	measure	fission	vision
glacier	glazier	Confucian	confusion

Sentences

3. It's a pleasure to see you, Mr. Shaw.
4. Could you give me directions to the Treasury Building?
5. After making an examination, the doctor will give his decision.
6. She wore a beige suit, and red shoes.

14. Consonants /f θ s š/

Words frequently used

Practice the following common words with the "*f* sound", /f/, as in *face*, the voiceless "*th* sound" /θ/, as in *thank*, the "*s* sound" /s/, as in *see*, and the "*sh* sound" /š/, as in *she*.

face	thank	see	she
five	thought	say	sure
office	nothing	possibly	special
before	mathematical	listen	direction
if	breath	nice	cash
life	south	place	wish

Sentences

7. They went to the cafeteria for some coffee.
8. I thought I'd go south, not north.
9. Did your sister send this to us?
10. Shall we wash our clothes, or brush them?

15. Consonants /v ð z ž/

Words frequently used

Practice the following common words containing the "*v* sound" /v/, as in *very*, the voiced "*th* sound" /ð/, as in *this*, the "*z* sound" /z/, as in *zoo*, or the "*zh* sound" /ž/, as in *measure*.

very	this	zoo	measure
visit	that	zero	vision
every	another	thousand	confusion
ever	rather	Tuesday	division
five	smooth	was	garage
have	bathe	always	rouge

Sentences

11. I live very near Avery Avenue.
12. My brothers did that themselves.
13. He always goes to the zoo on Thursdays.
14. I have to measure the garage.

16. *Consonants* /f v s z θ ð š ž/

Review sentences

Review the sentences you practiced in PD 26.

A. Sentences with /ž/

1. I have to measure the garage.
2. The collision occurred because of the driver's poor vision.

B. Sentences with /š/ and /ž/

3. It's a pleasure to see you, Mr. Shaw.
4. Could you give me directions to the Treasury Building?
5. After making an examination, the doctor will give his decision.
6. She wore a beige suit, and red shoes.

C. Sentences with /f/, /θ/, /s/, and /š/

7. They went to the cafeteria for some coffee.
8. I thought I'd go south, not north.
9. Did your sister send this to us?
10. Shall we wash our clothes, or brush them?

D. Sentences with /v/, /ð/, /z/, and /ž/

11. I live very near Avery Avenue.
12. My brothers did that themselves.
13. He always goes to the zoo on Thursdays.
14. I have to measure the garage.

Pronunciation Drill 27

17. *Consonants* /r l/

Words frequently used

The "*r* sound" in English may be made in several different ways. The "*r* sound" before a vowel may be made by turning the tip of the tongue up toward the palate. The tongue does not touch the palate, and it does not vibrate. The /r/ is voiced, like /d/.

The "*l* sound" before vowels, as in *leap*, is made with the front of the tongue touching the ridge just behind the teeth, and the middle of the tongue high. The "*l* sound" after vowels, as in *call*, is made with the tip of the tongue touching the ridge behind the teeth, and with the back of the tongue high. Some speakers have only one variety of *l*, the "back *l*", as in *call*, which they use everywhere.

Practice the following common words containing the "*r* sound" before vowels, /r/, as in *right*.

right	run	ready	wrap
read	real	red	restaurant
ring	rice	rock	rich
railroad	radio	wrote	really
room	rain	remind	rates

Sentences

1. It's raining rather hard today.
2. Are you ready to go, Robert?
3. Rachel's roommate is named Ruth.
4. Would you rather have a radio, or a record player?

18. *The Consonant* /l/

Words frequently used

Practice the following common words containing the "*l* sound" /l/, as in *let* and *call*.

let	look	eleven	well
like	low	million	all
last	lie	billion	feel
letter	law	hello	sell
late	lose	July	call

Sentences

5. We all like to get letters.
6. Carolyn lives on Lowell Lane.
7. Do you feel well today?
8. Does he like to look at television?

19. *Consonants* /l r/

Words in contrast

Now you will hear some pairs of words which differ in having the "*l* sound" /l/, as in *lie*, or the "*r* sound" /r/, as in *rye*. The first word has /l/; the second word has /r/.

lie	rye	line	Rhine	low	row	mull	myrrh
dill	deer	look	rook	lock	rock	lake	rake
list	wrist	light	right	lobe	robe	lid	rid
loss	Ross	lace	race	sill	seer	boll	bore
nil	near	pole	pour				

Sentences

9. Louise writes long letters to her father every Saturday.
10. We had a very long trip to Lexington, because we took the wrong road.
11. Does the bell ring regularly at four o'clock?
12. Robert Lane lives in a double room.

20. *Consonants* /l r/

Words in contrast

Now you will hear some other pairs of words which differ in having the "*l* sound" /l/, as in *lie*, or the "*r* sound" /r/, as in *rye*. Here the first word has /r/, and the second word has /l/.

rid	lid	raid	laid	royal	loyal	reach	leech
ruse	lose	rip	lip	wrap	lap	rot	lot
road	load	rest	lest	root	loot	rag	lag
rear	rill	gore	goal	mire	mile	tore	tall
room	loom	rain	lane				

Sentences

13. I like rare steak.
14. Rose didn't feel well yesterday.
15. Are you looking for a restaurant?
16. Remember to read lesson eleven.

21. *Consonants* /l r/

Review sentences

Review the sentences you practiced in PD 27.

A. Sentences with /r/

1. It's raining rather hard today.
2. Are you ready to go, Robert?
3. Rachel's roommate is named Ruth.
4. Would you rather have a radio, or a record player?

B. Sentences with /l/

5. We all like to get letters.
6. Carolyn lives on Lowell Lane.
7. Do you feel well today?
8. Does he like to look at television?

C. Sentences with /l/ and /r/

9. Louise writes long letters to her father every Saturday.
10. We had a very long trip to Lexington, because we took the wrong road.
11. Does the bell ring regularly at four o'clock?
12. Robert Lane lives in a double room.
13. I like rare steak.
14. Rose didn't feel well yesterday.
15. Are you looking for a restaurant?
16. Remember to read lesson eleven.

22. *Consonants* /m n ŋ/

Words frequently used

The "*m*, *n*, and *ng* sounds" are nasals. That is, in making these sounds, the mouth passage is closed at some point, and the nose passage is open. All these sounds are voiced, like /d/. The "*m* sound" is made by closing the lips and then opening them. The "*n* sound" is made by touching the tip of the tongue to the ridge just behind the upper teeth. The "*ng* sound" is made by touching the back of the tongue to the velum, or soft palate, behind the roof of the mouth.

Practice the following common words containing the "*m* sound" /m/, as in *much*.

much	Miss	summer	same
many	Mrs.	coming	some
maybe	Mr.	September	come
man	might	November	seem
morning	minute	December	time

Sentences

1. My mother goes to Maine every summer.
2. Maybe Mr. Manning lives on Maple Street.
3. How many women make this much money?
4. What time is it, Miss Hamilton?

23. *The Consonant* /n/

Words frequently used

Practice the following common words containing the "*n* sound" /n/, as in *need*.

need	seven	not	ten
nice	men	Sunday	fourteen
afternoon	women	Monday	in
evening	know	running	can
one	new	nine	then

Sentences

5. I need a new pen.
6. Do you know her name?
7. On Sunday evening, there's a concert at
   the National Gallery.
8. When can Mr. Nelson come?

24. *Consonants* /ŋ ŋg ŋk/

Words frequently used

The letters *ng* are pronounced /ŋ/, as in *long* and *singer*; they are pronounced /ŋg/, as in *finger* and *longer*. The letters *ng* are also pronounced /nj/, as in *stranger* and *ginger*. Notice that *-ng* is pronounced /ŋ/ at the end of a noun (*thing*) or a verb (*sing*) or a word derived from such a word (*singer*); it is also pronounced /ŋ/ at the end of adjectives (*long*).

-ng is pronounced /ŋg/ in words like *longer, longest, stronger* and *strongest*, and in words ending in *-ngle*, etc. (*single, bangle.*)

-nge is pronounced /nj/ at the end of words (*strange*), and in words derived from such words (*stranger*).

In English, the /ŋ/ never occurs at the beginning of words, and in standard English, /ŋg/ never occurs at the end of words.

Practice the following common words containing the "*ng* sound" /ŋ/, as in *thing*, the "*ngg* sound"/ŋg/, as in *younger*, and the "*nk* sound" /ŋk/, as in *bank*. Columns 1 and 2 below have words with /ŋ/, column 3 has words with /ŋg/, and column 4 has words with /ŋk/.

1	2	3	4
thing	bringing	younger	bank
young	singing	longer	think
song	ringing	single	pink
wrong	hanging	finger	thanking
sing	swinging	stronger	drinking

9. How long can you sing without getting tired?
10. Bill Browning always brings the morning paper.
11. This thing is stronger, and it will last longer.
12. I'm thinking of bringing my check to the bank.

25. *Consonants* /m n ŋ ŋg ŋk/

Words in contrast

Now you will hear some pairs or groups of words which differ in their nasal sound. Each word has one of the following: the "*m* sound" /m/, as in *ram*, the "*n* sound" /n/, as in *ran*, the "*ng* sound" /ŋ/, as in *rang*, the "*ngg* sound" /ŋg/, as in *wrangle*, or the "*nk* sound" /ŋk/, as in *rankle*.

mice nice	dime dine
sin sing	thin thing
rang ran ram	sinner singer
hang hangar anger	tan tang tank
ban bang bank	

kin king	Kim kin king
rum rung	rum run rung
singer finger	lawn long longer
hung hunger	bang banging bangle
thin thing think	

Sentences

13. Mr. Emerson sings tenor.
14. I'm drinking ginger ale, not orange juice.
15. *Kim* is the name of a novel by Kipling.
16. Is John going to New York next Sunday?

26. *Consonants* /mp nt nd nč/

Words frequently used

Practice the following common words containing the "*mp* sounds" /mp/, as in *lamp*, the "*nt* sounds" /nt/, as in *sent*, the "*nd* sounds" /nd/, as in *send*, and the "*nch* sounds" /nč/, as in *lunch*.

lamp	sent	send	lunch
sample	rent	rained	inch
damp	can't	spend	bench
campus	hunt	planned	branch

Sentences

17. This campus is damp in winter.
18. Many students rent rooms near DuPont Circle.
19. We planned to spend the day at the beach,
    but it rained.
20. He went to an empty bench.

27. *Consonants* /mp mb nd nt ŋ ŋg ŋk/

Words in contrast

Now you will hear some pairs and groups of words which differ in having the "*mp* sounds" /mp/, as in *simple*, the "*mb* sounds" /mb/, as in *symbol*, the "*nd* sounds" /nd/, as in *send*, the "*nt* sounds" /nt/, as in *sent*, the "*ng* sounds" /ŋ/, as in *thing*, the *ngg* sounds" /ŋg/, as in *finger*, or the "*ngk* sounds" /ŋk/, as in *think*.

simple symbol	ramp ramble
sent send	pained paint
can't canned	hang angle ankle
rang wrangle rankle	sing single sink
ample amble	bend bent
lent lend	faint feigned
mound mount	

Sentences

21. The children in camp rambled through the woods.
22. That letter can't be sent until it's signed.
23. On her way to the bank, Mrs. Young hurt her ankle.
24. The tree bent in the wind.

28. *Consonants* /m n ŋ mp nt nd nč mb ŋg ŋk/

Review sentences

Review the sentences you practiced in PD 28.

A. Sentences with /m/

1. My mother goes to Maine every summer.
2. Maybe Mr. Manning lives on Maple Street.
3. How many women make this much money?
4. What time is it, Miss Hamilton?

B. Sentences with /n/

5. I need a new pen.
6. Do you know her name?
7. On Sunday evening, there's a concert at the National Gallery.
8. When can Mr. Nelson come?

C. Sentences with /ŋ ŋg ŋk/

9. How long can you sing without getting tired?
10. Bill Browning always brings the morning paper.
11. This thing is stronger, and it will last longer.
12. I'm thinking of bringing my check to the bank.

D. Sentences with /m n ŋ ŋg ŋk/

13. Mr. Emerson sings tenor.
14. I'm drinking ginger ale, not orange juice.
15. *Kim* is the name of a novel by Kipling.
16. Is John going to New York next Sunday?

E. Sentences with /mp nt nd nč/

17. This campus is damp in winter.
18. Many students rent rooms near DuPont Circle.
19. We planned to spend the day at the beach, but it rained.
20. He went to an empty bench.

F. Sentences with /mp mb nt nd ŋ ŋk/

21. The children in camp rambled through the woods.
22. That letter can't be sent until it's signed.
23. On her way to the bank, Mrs. Young hurt her ankle.
24. The tree bent in the wind.

GROUP XII
Consonant Clusters

Pronunciation Drill 29

1. s Clusters

Words frequently used

Remember that /s/ is voiceless. Be careful not to make it voiced when it is followed by a voiced consonant.

Practice the following common words containing the "*sl* sounds" /sl/, as in *slow*, and the "*sw* sounds" /sw/, as in *sweet*.

slow	slot	sweet	swell
sleep	slang	swallow	swing
slip	slippery	swim	Sweden
slice	Slavic	swear	sweetheart

Sentences
1. Swim to shore slowly.
2. Miss Sweeney is sleeping.

2. *Consonants* /st sts/

Words frequently used

Practice the following common words containing the "*st* sounds" /st/, as in *steak*, and the "*sts* sounds", /sts/, as in *lasts*.

steak	Mister (Mr.)	fast	lasts
student	sister	lost	rests
star	yesterday	least	tastes
stand	western	rest	tests

Sentences

3. My sister is a student at Western Reserve University.
4. Mr. Steel always rests after running fast.

3. *Consonants* /sk sks/

Words frequently used

Practice the following common words containing the "*sk* sounds" /sk/, as in *skin*, and the "*sks* sounds" /sks/, as in *desks*.

skin	scold	escape	desks
sky	skate	ask	risks
school	skip	desk	asks

Sentences

5. There are ten desks in the school room.
6. Ask Mr. Skinner if we can skate here.

4. *Consonants* /sp sps/

Words frequently used

Practice the following common words containing the "*sp* sounds" /sp/, as in *speak*, and the "*sps* sounds" /sps/, as in *gasps*.

speak	speed	especially	gasps
space	spend	expensive	grasps
special	spelling	hospital	wasps

Sentences

7. We don't eat spinach with a spoon.
8. This hospital is especially good.

5. *Consonants* /skr str/

Practice the following common words containing the "*skr* sounds" /skr/, as in *scream*, and the "*str* sounds" /str/, as in *street*.

scream	scrub	street	stranger
scrambled	Scranton	string	strong
scratch	describe	stress	destroy
screen	description	straight	instructions

Sentences

9. I want scrambled eggs, please.
10. All the streets in this town are straight.

6. *Consonants* /spr spl šr/

Words frequently used

Practice the following common words containing the "*spr* sounds" /spr/, as in *spring*, the "*spl* sounds" /spl/, as in *splendid*, and the "*shr* sounds" /šr/, as in *shrub*.

spring	splendid	shrub
sprang	splash	shrimp
bed spread	splinter	shrink
spray	splatter	shrine

Sentences

11. Today is a splendid spring day.
12. Shrimp is my favorite seafood.

7. *Consonants* /sm sn/

Words frequently used

Practice the following common words containing the "*sm* sounds" /sm/, as in *smoke*, or the "*sn* sounds" /sn/, as in *snow*.

smoke	smell	snow	sniff
Smith	smooth	snake	snip
smile	smart	snap	snack
small	smash	sneezing	snob

Sentences

13. Do you smell smoke, Mr. Snow?
14. The Smiths are in the snack bar.

8. *s Clusters*

Review

Review the sentences you have practiced in PD 29.

A. Sentences with /sl/ and /sw/

1. Swim to shore slowly.
2. Miss Sweeney is sleeping.

B. Sentences with /st/ and /sts/

3. My sister is a student at Western Reserve University.
4. Mr. Steel always rests after running fast.

C. Sentences with /sk/ and /sks/

5. There are ten desks in the school room.
6. Ask Mr. Skinner if we can skate here.

D. Sentences with /sp/ and /sps/

    7. We don't eat spinach with a spoon.
    8. This hospital is especially good.

E. Sentences with /skr/ and /str/

    9. I want scrambled eggs, please.
   10. All the streets in this town are straight.

F. Sentences with /spr/, /spl/, and /šr/

   11. Today is a splendid spring day.
   12. Shrimp is my favorite seafood.

G. Sentences with /sm/ and /sn/

   13. Do you smell smoke, Mr. Snow?
   14. The Smiths are in the snack bar.

Consonant Clusters

Pronunciation Drill 30

1. /pl pr kl kr bl br/

Words frequently used

Practice the following common words containing the "*pl* sounds" /pl/, as in *please*, or the "*pr* sounds" /pr/, as in *probably*.

please	airplane	probably	previous
place	employ	price	April
plan	unpleasant	practice	improve
plenty	apply	professor	approve

Sentences

1. Please find out what time the plane leaves.
2. We'll probably see Professor White in April.

2. *Consonants* /pl pr/

Words in contrast

Now you will hear some pairs of words which differ in having the "*pl* sounds" /pl/, as in *play*, or the "*pr* sounds" /pr/, as in *pray*. The first word has /pl/; the second word has /pr/.

play pray		plowed proud
plank prank		plod prod
plays praise		applies apprise
ply pry		plied pride
plate prate		plow prow
plies prize		pleasant present

Sentences

3. They plan to practice tonight.
4. What's the price of these pretty plates?

3. *Consonants* /kl kr/

Words frequently used

Practice the following common words containing the "*kl* sounds" /kl/, as in *class*, or the "*kr* sounds" /kr/, as in *cross*.

class	close (v.)	cross	crazy
clean	close (a.)	cream	across
club	climate	cracker	crowd
closet	clothing	criminal	cry

Sentences

5. In this climate, you need warm clothing.
6. He went across the street to buy some ice cream.

4. *Consonants* /kl kr/

Words in contrast

Now you will hear some pairs of words which differ in having the "*kl* sounds" /kl/, as in *clown*, or the "*kr* sounds" /kr/, as in *crown*. The first word has /kl/; the second word has /kr/.

clown	crown	Clyde	cried	clamp	cramp
clack	crack	clabber	crabber	class	crass
cloak	croak	clash	crash	clue	crew
clank	crank	close	crows	clam	cram
climb	crime	click	crick		

Sentences

7. On a clear day, we can see across the valley.
8. Was the club house crowded last night?

106

5. *Consonants* /bl br/

Words frequently used

Practice the following common words containing the "*bl* sounds" /bl/, as in *black*, or the "*br* sounds" /br/, as in *brown*.

black	blood	brown	bread
blue	blind	breakfast	brother
blow	blink	bring	break
blank	blame	brave	breath

Sentences

9. The Blanding School colors are blue and black.
10. Bring my brother's breakfast, please.

6. *Consonants* /bl br/

Words in contrast

Now you will hear some pairs of words which differ in having the "*bl* sounds" /bl/, as in *blue*, or the "*br* sounds" /br/, as in *brew*. The first word has /bl/; the second word has /br/.

blue	brew	bland	brand
Blake	break	blackish	brackish
blain	brain	blush	brush
blazon	brazen	blest	breast
blight	bright	blouse	browse
blink	brink	bled	bread
blaze	braise	blade	braid
blanch	branch	blandish	brandish
bleach	breach	bleed	breed
bloom	broom	blues	bruise

Sentences

11. My brother bought black shoes, and a brown hat.
12. Today the wind is blowing, and the sun is shining brightly.

7. *Consonants* /pl pr kl kr bl br/

Review sentences

Review the sentences you practiced in PD 30.

A. Sentences with /pl/ and /pr/

1. Please find out what time the plane leaves.
2. We'll probably see Professor White in April.
3. They plan to practice tonight.
4. What's the price of these pretty plates?

B. Sentences with /kl/ and /kr/

5. In this climate, you need warm clothing.
6. He went across the street to buy some ice cream.
7. On a clear day, we can see across the valley.
8. Was the club house crowded last night?

C. Sentences with /bl/ and /br/

9. The Blanding School colors are blue and black.
10. Bring my brother's breakfast, please.
11. My brother bought black shoes, and a brown hat.
12. Today the wind is blowing, and the sun is shining brightly.

Pronunciation Drill 31

8. *Consonants* /gl gr fl fr/

Words frequently used

Practice the following common words containing the "*gl* sounds"
/gl/, as in *glad*, or the "*gr* sounds" /gr/, as in *great*.

glad	glorious	great	grow
glass	globe	green	ground
glove	glue	grass	group

1. Was Gloria glad to see you?
2. The grass is very green now.

9. *Consonants* /gl gr/

Words in contrast

Now you will hear some words which differ in having the "*gl* sounds" /gl/, as in *glue*, or the "*gr* sounds" /gr/, as in *grew*. The first word has /gl/; the second word has /gr/.

glass	grass	glue	grew	glow	grow
glade	grade	gland	grand	glaze	graze
gloom	groom	glad	grad	glean	green
				glimmer	grimmer

Sentences
3. I'm glad the grass is growing.
4. That group of students is from Glasgow.

10. *Consonants* /fl fr/

Words frequently used

Practice the following common words containing the "*fl* sounds" /fl/, as in *flag*, or the "*fr* sounds" /fr/, as in *free*.

flag	float	free	from
flat	floor	France	front
fly	flower	fresh	fruit

Sentences

5. This seaplane flies, and also floats on the water.
6. Do you prefer fresh fruit, or frozen fruit?

11. *Consonants* /fl fr/

Now you will hear some pairs of words which differ in having the "*fl* sounds" /fl/, as in *flee*, or the "*fr* sounds" /fr/, as in *free*. The first word has /fl/; the second word has /fr/.

flee	free	flesh	fresh	fly	fry	flute	fruit
flank	frank	flail	frail	flame	frame	flay	fray
fleas	freeze	flier	frier	flight	fright	flow	fro
flock	frock	flog	frog				

Sentences

7. Which flag is flying in front of the embassy?
8. Fred and Florence are from Florida.

12. *Consonants* /gl gr fl fr/

Review sentences

Review the sentences you practiced in PD 31.

A. Sentences with /gl/ and /gr/

1. Was Gloria glad to see you?
2. The grass is very green now.
3. I'm glad the grass is growing.
4. That group of students is from Glasgow.

B. Sentences with /fl/ and /fr/

5. This seaplane flies, and also floats on the water.
6. Do you prefer fresh fruit, or frozen fruit?
7. Which flag is flying in front of the embassy?
8. Fred and Florence are from Florida.

110

13. *Consonants* /tr θr dr/

Words frequently used

Practice the following common words with the "*tr* sounds" /tr/, as in *tree*, the "voiceless *th* and *r* sounds" /θr/, as in *three*, and the "*dr* sounds" /dr/, as in *drive*.

tree	three	drive
true	through	drink
try	throw	dress
train	thread	drop

Sentences

1. It's a two-hour trip by train.
2. Did the boys throw the ball through the window?
3. Please drive me to the drugstore.

14. *Consonants* /tr θr/

Words in contrast

Now you will hear some pairs of words which differ in having the "*tr* sounds" /tr/, as in *tree*, or the "voiceless *th* and *r* sounds" /θr/, as in *three*. The first word has /tr/; the second word has /θr/.

tree	three	trash	thrash
trice	thrice	true	threw
trip	thrip	tread	thread
trill	thrill	trust	thrust

Sentences

4. He took a trip through three states.
5. Try to put the thread through the eye of the needle.
6. Mr. Truman's business is thriving.

15. *Consonant Clusters*

Supplementary Words

You have now studied the consonant clusters which appear most frequently at the beginning and in the middle of words in English. Below are words containing consonant clusters which are used less frequently in the same way.

The "*py* sound."   SAY: Pure, pew, putrid, pewter.
The "*tw* sound."   SAY: Twin, twine, twist, twenty.
The "*ky* sound."   SAY: Cute, curious, cure.
The "*kw* sound."   SAY: Quick, quiet, quit, quaint.
The "*by* sound."   SAY: Beautiful, beauty, bureau, bugle.
The "*dw* sound."   SAY: Dwarf, dwindle, dwell.
The "*fy* sound."   SAY: Few, futile, feud.
The "*thw* sound."   SAY: Thwart.
The "*hy* sound."   SAY: Hue, huge, humid.
The "*spy* sound."   SAY: Spew, sputum, spume.
The "*skl* sound."   SAY: Sclerosis.
The "*sky* sound."   SAY: Skewer, askew.
The "*skw* sound."   SAY: Squeeze, squeak, squabble.

GROUP XIV

R Followed by a Consonant

Pronunciation Drill 33

1. *Consonants* /rp rt rč rk/

Words frequently used

The "*r* sound" followed by a consonant occurs in the middle and at the end of English words. If time permits, review pages 32-38, where vowels before *r* are given.

Practice the following common words containing the "*rp* sounds" /rp/, as in *sharp*, the "*rt* sounds" /rt/, as in *heart*, the "*rch* sounds" /rč/, as in *church*, and the "*rk* sounds" /rk/, as in *work*.

sharp	heart	church	work
purple	dirty	search	fork
Antwerp	porch	March	circle
Harper	part	arch	parking

Sentences

1. Please sharpen this purple pencil.
2. Bert spilled dessert on his shirt at the party.
3. Many churches have Gothic arches.
4. Does Mark work in New York?

2. *Consonants* /rb rd rg rj/

Words frequently used

Practice the following common words containing the "*rb* sounds" /rb/, as in *barber*, the "*rd* sounds" /rd/, as in *word*, the "*rg* sounds" /rg/, as in *Pittsburgh*, and the "*rj* sounds" /rj/, as in *urge*.

barber	word	Pittsburgh	urge
harbor	heard	iceberg	large
suburb	third	cargo	charge
absorb	cured	target	sergeant

Sentences

5. Is there a barber shop in this suburb?
6. I heard every word you said.
7. The ship hit an iceberg, and the cargo sank.
8. Does the sergeant have a large car?

3. *Consonants* /rf rθ rv rð/

Words frequently used

Practice the following common words containing the "*rf* sounds" /rf/, as in *careful*, the "*r* voiceless *th* sounds" /rθ/, as in *fourth*, the "*rv* sounds" /rv/, as in *curve*, and the "*r* voiced *th* sounds" /rð/, as in *further*.

careful	fourth	curve	further
orphan	earth	serve	farther
scarf	birth	deserve	farthest
perfect	north	nerve	northern

Sentences

9. The scarf matches perfectly.
10. His birthplace was North Carolina.
11. Does it make you nervous when a car goes around a curve too fast?
12. Northern New York is farther from here than you think.

4. *Consonants* /rs rš rz rž/

Words frequently used

Practice the following common words containing the "*rs* sounds" /rs/, as in *person*, the "*rsh* sounds" /rš/ as in *harsh*, the "*rz* sounds" /rz/, as in *stairs*, and the "*rzh* sounds" /rž/, as in *Persia*.

person	harsh	stairs	Persia
worse	marsh	hers	Persian
nurse	partial	Thursday	version
horse	portion	cars	aversion

114

13. A person who writes verse is called a poet.
14. Have you heard of the Marshall Plan?
15. Are these cars *both* hers?
16. Does he speak Persian?

5. *Consonants* /rl rm rn/

Words frequently used

Practice the following common words containing the "*rl* sounds" /rl/, as in *girl*, the "*rm* sounds" /rm/, as in *arm*, and the "*rn* sounds" /rn/, as in *learn*.

girl	arm	learn
curl	permanent	turn
early	storm	modern
Arlington	farm	morning

Sentences

17. Does the girl have curly hair?
18. Will they live on the farm permanently?
19. What did you learn this morning?

6. *R Followed by a Consonant*

Review Sentences

Review the sentences you practiced in PD 33.

A. Sentences with /rp/, /rt/, /rč/, and /rk/

1. Please sharpen this purple pencil.
2. Bert spilled dessert on his shirt at the party.
3. Many churches have Gothic arches.
4. Does Mark work in New York?

B. Sentences with /rb/, /rd/, /rg/, and /rj/

    5. Is there a barber shop in this suburb?
    6. I heard every word you said.
    7. The ship hit an iceberg, and the cargo sank.
    8. Does the sergeant have a large car?

C. Sentences with /rf/, /rθ/, /rv/, and /rð/

    9. This scarf matches perfectly.
  10. His birthplace was North Carolina.
  11. Does it make you nervous when a car goes around a curve too fast?
  12. Northern New York is farther from here than you think.

D. Sentences with /rs/, /rš/, /rz/, /rž/

  13. A person who writes verse is called a poet.
  14. Have you heard of the Marshall Plan?
  15. Are these cars *both* hers?
  16. Does he speak Persian?

E. Sentences with /rl/, /rm/, /rn/

  17. Does the girl have curly hair?
  18. Will they live on the farm permanently?
  19. What did you learn this morning?

116

GROUP XV

Final Consonant Clusters

Pronunciation Drill 34

1. *Consonants* /ps ts fs θs pt kt ft st št čt/

Words frequently used

NOTE: Review pages 39-44 before doing this lesson.

Below are some nouns ending in /ps/, /ts/, /ks/, /fs/, and /θs/, in their possessive and plural forms, made by adding the "*s* sound" to the singular form of the noun. Practice these words containing final consonant clusters.

caps	streets	backs	coughs
maps	coats	books	berths
cups	dates	wife's*	Ruth's
shops	weeks	handkerchiefs	breaths
minutes	thanks	laughs	deaths

Sentences

1. These shops don't sell maps.
2. She's always at least ten minutes late for dates.
3. Thanks for the books.
4. Those are my wife's handkerchiefs.
5. Ruth's job is recording the births and deaths in this city.

*Most nouns ending in /f/ form their plural by changing /f/ to /v/, and adding /z/.

117

2. Consonants /ps ts ks fs/

Words frequently used

Below are some verbs ending in /ps/, /ts/, /ks/, and /fs/, in the third person singular present tense form, made by adding the "s sound" to the simple form of the verb.* Practice these words containing the final consonant clusters.

stops	writes	takes	laughs
keeps	sits	checks	coughs
sleeps	lets	makes	stuffs
hopes	gets	talks	telegraphs

Sentences

6. He usually stops work at noon, and sleeps for an hour.
7. She sits in the park every day, and waits for her friend.
8. He always walks and talks with me.
9. She always laughs at us.

*Verbs ending in /θ/, such as *froth*, also form the third person singular present tense form by adding /s/, but such verbs are rare.

3. Consonants /pt kt ft/

Words frequently used

Below are some verbs ending in /pt/, /kt/, and /ft/, in their past tense form, made in regular verbs by adding the "t sound" to the simple form of the verb. ** Remember that although regular verbs add the letters -ed to form the past tense, the pronunciation is /t/, when the verb ends in /p/, /k/, or /f/. Practice the words below ending in final consonant clusters.

**Verbs ending in /θ/, such as *froth*, also form the past tense by adding /t/, but such verbs are rare.

118

stopped	talked	laughed
hoped	liked	coughed
kept	walked	left
slept	looked	telegraphed

Sentences

10. They stopped in Chicago and slept.
11. We checked our suitcases at the station, and walked around the city.
12. I wonder why he laughed when he left.

4. *Consonants* /st št čt/

Words frequently used

Below are some verbs ending in /st/, /št/, and /čt/, in their past tense form. Practice these words containing final consonant clusters.

passed	finished	watched
danced	wished	reached
noticed	rushed	touched
missed	cashed	scratched

Sentences

13. They danced until midnight.
14. I finished my homework at nine o'clock.
15. We watched television last night.

5. *Final Consonant Clusters*

Review Sentences

Review the sentences you have practiced in PD 34.

A. Sentences with /ps/, /ts/, /ks/, and /θs/

1. These shops don't sell maps.

2. She's always at least ten minutes late
   for dates.
3. Thanks for the books.
4. Those are my wife's handkerchiefs.
5. Ruth's job is recording the births and
   deaths in this city.
6. Mr. Brown usually stops work at noon,
   and sleeps for an hour.
7. She sits in the park every day, and
   waits for her friend.
8. He always walks and talks with me.
9. She always laughs at us.

B. Sentences with /pt/, /kt/, and /ft/

10. They stopped in Chicago and slept.
11. We checked our suitcase at the station,
    and walked around the city.
12. I wonder why he laughed when he left.

C. Sentences with /st/, /št/, and /čt/

13. They danced until midnight.
14. I finished my homework at nine
    o'clock.
15. We watched television last night.

Pronunciation Drill 35

6. Consonants /bz dz gz vz ðz/

Words frequently used

Below are some nouns ending in /bz/, /dz/, /gz/, /vz/, and
/ðz/, in their possessive and plural forms, regularly made by
adding the "z sound" to the singular form of the noun. Practice
these words containing final consonant clusters.

cabs	Ed's	dogs	wives	paths
clubs	beds	eggs	leaves	baths
jobs	heads	legs	knives	
Bob's	roads	drugs	lives	

Sentences

1. Bob's sister has two jobs.
2. These beds are more comfortable than Ed's.
3. Both the dog's legs are hurt.
4. Mr. Ives and Mr. Cleaves have been friends all their lives.
5. Does the new house have two baths?

7. *Consonants* /lz mz nz ŋz rz/

Words frequently used

Below are some nouns ending in /lz/, /mz/, /nz/, /ŋz/, and /rz/, in their possessive and plural forms, made by adding the "z sound" to the singular form of the nouns. Practice these words containing final consonant clusters.

names	nouns	things	pencils
Jim's	Janes'	rings	cars
times	pens	walls	ears
poems	songs	smiles	letters
towns	king's	schools	chairs

Sentences

6. How many times have you played these games?
7. These signs say there are telephones in this drugstore.
8. What are the king's favorite songs?
9. The walls of these schools are made of brick.
10. Do you get many letters from your sisters and brothers?

8. *Consonants* /bz dz gz vz ðz/

Words frequently used

Below are some verbs ending in /bz/, /dz/, /gz/, /vz/, and /ðz/, in the third person singular, present tense form. Practice these words containing final consonant clusters.

robs	decides	believes
rubs	rides	lives
describes	digs	leaves
grabs	brags	arrives
leads	begs	breathes
reads	hugs	bathes
		smooths

Sentences

11. This book describes Washington, D. C.
12. He sometimes reads while he rides on the bus.
13. Every day, John begs us to go with him.
14. The teacher always gives him a book when he arrives.
15. He usually bathes at nine o'clock.

9. *Final Consonant Clusters*

Review sentences

Review the sentences you have practiced in PD 35.

A. Sentences with /bz/, /dz/, /gz/, /vz/, and /ðz/ in nouns

1. Bob's sister has two jobs.
2. These beds are more comfortable than Ed's.
3. Both the dog's legs are hurt.
4. Mr. Ives and Mr. Cleaves have been friends all their lives.
5. Does the new house have two baths?

B. Sentences with /lz/, /mz/, /nz/, /ŋz/ and /rz/ in nouns

6. How many times have you played these games?
7. These signs say there are telephones in this drugstore.
8. What are the king's favorite songs?
9. The walls of these schools are made of brick.
10. Do you get many letters from your sisters and brothers?

C. Sentences with /bz/, /dz/, /gz/, /vz/, and /ðz/

11. This book describes Washington, D. C.
12. He sometimes reads while he rides on the bus.
13. Every day, John begs us to go with him.
14. The teacher always gives him a book when he arrives.
15. He usually bathes at nine o'clock.

Pronunciation Drill 36

10. *Consonants* /mz nz ŋz lz rz/

Words frequently used

Below are some verbs ending in /mz/, /nz/, /ŋz/, /lz/, and /rz/, in the third person singular, present tense form. Practice these words containing final consonant clusters.

comes	runs	sings	falls	wears
seems	begins	rings	feels	hears
dreams	cleans	brings	pulls	appears
screams	turns	bangs	smiles	interferes

Sentences
1. It seems that he always comes to class late.
2. The class begins at nine o'clock.
3. The postman always rings the doorbell when he brings us letters.
4. Ask him how he feels today.
5. She always hears the news on the radio.

11. *Consonants* /bd jd gd vd ðd/

Words frequently used

Below are some verbs ending in /bd/, /jd/, /gd/, /vd/, and /ðd/, in the past tense form. Practice these words containing final consonant clusters.

robbed	engaged	lagged	believed	breathed
rubbed	judged	bragged	lived	bathed
grabbed	urged	begged	received	smoothed
described	obliged	hugged	arrived	

Sentences

6. This criminal robbed a bank.
7. Dr. Black charged $5.00 for that treatment.
8. We begged them to stay with us.
9. He received the letter when he arrived.
10. She stood beside the window, and breathed the fresh air.

12. *Consonants* /md nd ŋd/

Words frequently used

Below are some verbs ending in /md/, /nd/, and /ŋd/, in the past tense form. Practice these words ending in consonant clusters.

seemed	turned
dreamed	rained
named	longed (for)
warmed	belonged
learned	clanged
cleaned	banged

11. They seemed to enjoy the movie very much.
12. He learned English when he returned to the United States.
13. The little boy banged the door.

13. *Consonants* /zd ld rd/

Words frequently used

Below are some verbs ending in /zd/, /ld/, and /rd/, in their past tense form. Practice these words containing final consonant clusters.

advised	called	heard
closed	pulled	appeared
amazed	killed	cleared
surprised	smiled	lowered

Sentences

14. I closed the door because I supposed you had gone.
15. Robert called for Louise at eight o'clock.
16. I heard every word you said.

14. *Final Consonant Clusters*

Review sentences

Review the sentences you have practiced in PD 36.

A. Sentences with /mz/, /nz/, /ŋz/, /lz/, and /rz/

1. It seems that he always comes to class late.
2. The class begins at nine o'clock.
3. The postman always rings the doorbell when he brings us letters.
4. Ask him how he feels today.
5. She always hears the news on the radio.

B. Sentences with /bd/, /jd/, /gd/, /vd/, and /ðd/

6. This criminal robbed a bank.
7. Dr. Black charged $5.00 for that treatment.
8. We begged them to stay with us.
9. He received the letter when he arrived.
10. She stood beside the window, and breathed the fresh air.

C. Sentences with /md/, /nd/, and /ŋd/

11. They seemed to enjoy the movie very much.
12. He learned English when he returned to the United States.
13. The little boy banged the door.

D. Sentences with /zd/, /ld/, and /rd/

14. I closed the door, because I supposed you had gone.
15. Robert called for Louise at eight o'clock.
16. I heard every word you said.

Pronunciation Drill 37
The Alphabet

Review the forms of the *capital letters*, *small letters*, and *names of the letters* of the English alphabet.

Capital Letter	Small Letter	Name of Letter
A	a	/ey/
B	b	/biy/
C	c	/siy/
D	d	/diy/
E	e	/iy/
F	f	/ef/
G	g	/jiy/
H	h	/eyč/
I	i	/ay/
J	j	/jey/
K	k	/key/
L	l	/el/
M	m	/em/

Capital Letter	Small Letter	Name of Letter
N	n	/en/
O	o	/ow/
P	p	/piy/
Q	q	/kyuw/
R	r	/aɾ/
S	s	/es/
T	t	/tiy/
U	u	/yuw/
V	v	/viy/
W	w	/dəbᵻlyùw/
X	x	/eks/
Y	y	/way/
Z	z	/ziy/
		(British /zed/)

1. REPEAT THE CAPITAL LETTERS.
2. REPEAT THE SMALL LETTERS.
3. THEN SAY THE ALPHABET BACKWARDS.
4. LISTEN TO THE ALPHABET SONG WHICH AMERICAN CHILDREN SING.

A B D C E F G
H I J K L M N O P
Q and R and S and T
U V W X Y Z
Now you've heard my ABC's
Won't you say them for me please.

Uses Of The Names Of The Letters

There are various occasions when it is necessary to use the names of the letters, and their plurals. The plural of a letter of the alphabet is usually written ´s (apostrophe - s /əpástrəfiy és/.) The plural s is pronounced /s, z, ɨz/ according to the last sound of the singular. SAY the following plurals:

/s/   f - f's
/ɨz/   h - h's, s - s's, x - x's,
/z/   a - a's, b's, c's, d's, e's, g's, i's, j's, k's,
     l's, m's, n's, o's, p's, q's, r's, t's, u's, v's,
     w's, y's, z's

Sentences

1. My teacher gave me three *a*'s and two *b*'s for my work in class.
2. *MISSISSIPPI* is spelled with four *s*'s and two *p*'s.
3. His name is John Doe - capital *j-o-h-n*, capital *d-o-e*.
4. The vowel-letters are *a, e, i, o, u,* and sometimes *y* and *w*.
5. The following are the consonant letters: *b c d, f g h, j k l m n, p q r s t, v w x y z.*

Use Of The Alphabet In Abbreviations

There are three common types of abbreviations in English:

1. The *Mr.* type of abbreviation (Pronunciation of abbreviation pronunciation of complete form)

Abbreviation	*Pronunciation*	*Full Form*
Mr.	/mĭstər/	Mister
Dr.	/dáktər/	Doctor
Maj.	/méyjər/	Major
Jr.	/júwnyər/	Junior
Dept.	/dipártmɨnt/	Department
Ave.	/ǽvɨnyuw/	Avenue
Mrs.	/mĭsɨz/	(Mistress)
lb., lbs.	/páwnd-z/	pound(s)
oz.	/áwns-ɨz/	ounce(s)

Mistress is never used as a title now, although it was a few hundred years ago, and Mrs. is pronounced /mĭsɨz/ by many people, /mĭzɨz/ or /miz/ by others. The abbreviations *lb.* and *oz.* are really abbreviations of non-English words.

2. The *UNESCO* type of abbreviation
(The abbreviation is pronounced like a word.)

Abbreviation	*Pronunciation*	*Full Form*
UNESCO	/yunéskow/	United Nations Educational, Scientific, and Cultural Organization
WAC	/wæk/	The Women's Army Corps
CARE	/kehr/	The Co-operative for American Remittances to Europe
ARAMCO	/ərǽmkow/	Arabian-American Oil Co.

3. The *M. D.* type of abbreviation

(Pronunciation of abbreviation-Names of letters in abbreviation.)

Abbreviation	*Pronunciation*	*Full Form*
M.D.	/em dǐy/	Medicinae Doctor
B.A.	/biy ey/	Bachelor of Arts
B.S.	/biy es/	Bachelor of Science
M.A.	/em éy/	Master of Arts
Ph.D.	/piy eyč dǐy/	Philosophiae Doctor
YMCA	/way em siy ey/	Young Men's Christian Association
APO	/ey piy ów/	Army Post Office
TVA	/tiy viy ey/	Tennessee Valley Authority
TWA	/tiy dəbil yuw ey/	Trans-World Airlines
CBS	/siy biy es/	Columbia Broadcasting System
NBC	/en biy siy/	National Broadcasting Company
C.I.O.	/siy ay ów/	Congress of Industrial Organizations
N.A.M.	/en ey ém/	National Association of Manufacturers
ICA	/ay siy ey/	International Cooperation Administration

The twenty-six letters of the English alphabet are used to represent the twenty-four consonant sounds and a minimum of fourteen vowel sounds. The following are some important things to know about how English spelling corresponds to English pronunciation.

1. The short vowel sounds are regularly represented by VC(C).

   back   pet   tip   knot   us

To represent the short vowel sound when you add a suffix beginning with a vowel (for example, -ing, -er, -est), double the final consonant letter if the word ends in one consonant.

   pat, patting   pet, petting   tip, tipping   knot, knotted

No spelling changes are made if the word ends in two consonants.

   back, backer   bend, bending   tick, ticking   knock, knocking
   rust, rusty

2. The long vowels are regularly represented by VC*e*.

   bake   Pete   type   note   use

Such words regularly lose the final *e* before a suffix beginning with a vowel.

   bake, baking   type, typist,   note, noted   use, using

(The long vowels are also represented by other spellings. See PD 38.)

3. Words which end in (C)*y*, change the *y* to *i* before the ending -*es*.

   baby, babies   city, cities   family, families   try, tries
   fly, flies

4. English spelling often uses two or more letters to represent one sound or no sound. (The letters in parentheses represent a single sound.)

(CH, TCH)	cheap	each	match
(CK)	pick	lack	lock
(DG-E)	bridge	judging	
(GH)	cough	enough	through
	bough	ought	thorough
(GN)	gnat	gnaw	sign
(KN)	knife	knock	
(MB)	comb	lamb	
(NG)	sing	singer	
(PH)	phone	philosophy	graph
(SH)	ship	fish	
(SI, SU)	measure	vision	
(SSI, TI)	mission	nation	
(TH)/ð/	then	mother bathe smooth	
(TH)/θ/	thin	mathematical truth	
(WR)	wrong	awry	write

The Alphabet And The Vowel Sounds Of English

You have studied the twenty vowel sounds represented by the five vowel letters, alone and in combination, as in the words below.

1	2	3	4
/i/ pit	/iy/ Pete		/ih/ peer
/e/ pet	/ey/ pate		/eh/ pare
/æ/ pat			
/ə/ putt			/əh/ purr
/a/ pot	/ay/ pie	/aw/ bout	/ah/ par
/ɔ/ dog			
/u/ put		/uw/ boot	/uh/ poor
/o/ port	/oy/ boy	/ow/ boat	/oh/ pour

All these vowel sounds are in loud stressed syllables.

In quiet unstressed syllables, the two most common vowel sounds are:

"the short *u* sound" /ə/ as in *butter*; and
"the barred-*i* sound" /ɨ/ as in *children, little, roses, just a minute*

The "barred-*i* sound" (represented by the letter *i* and a bar -, superimposed) is extremely frequent.

children	/čĭldrĭn/ or /čăldrĭn/
roses	/rówzĭz/
just a minute	/jĭst ə mĭnĭt/

The Alphabet And The Consonant Sounds Of English

The twenty-one consonant letters of the English alphabet are used alone, and in the combinations you studied on page 130 - 131, to represent the twenty-four consonant sounds. These sounds are represented by different symbols in different books (θ, th; đ. th, dh, ð; sh; zh, ž; ch, č, f; j, ğ, dz; ng, ŋ, etc.). The symbols are not important, if you can say and understand the sounds perfectly.

In each key word below, the letters which represent one of the twenty-four English consonant sounds are underlined.

The Consonant Sounds of English

/p/	apple	/t/	little	/č/	kitchen	/k/	pickle
/b/	rubber	/d/	body	/j/	ajar	/g/	bigger

/f/	telephone	/θ/	ether	/s/	classify	/š/	nation
/v/	ever	/ð/	mother	/z/	easy	/ž/	vision

/m/	grammar	/n/	banana	/y/	Malaya	/ŋ/	singer

/w/	away	/l/ /r/	early			/h/	rehearse

Pronunciation Drill 38

English spelling is irregular, especially the spelling of the vowel sounds. All spelling rules have exceptions, and these exceptions often occur in words which are frequently used. In the following lessons, you will study the spelling of the short and long vowel sounds, of the vowel sounds, of the vowel sounds before *r*, and of the consonants.

NOTE: (*c*) means consonant, and (*v*) means vowel.

1. *The Short And Long i Sounds*

The spelling of the "short *i* sound" /i/, as in *pit*, and the "long *i* sound" /ay/, as in *bite*.

The "short *i* sound" /i/, is regularly spelled *i(c)*.

> bit quit fin sit did tip

It is sometimes spelled *y*.

> rhythm mystery myth

The "long *i* sound" /ay/, is regularly spelled *i(c)e*, *y*, *y(c)e*, *ie*, or *igh*.

> bite quite fine; by cry type; die lie; high night

This sound is often spelled *y* when it is final in words of one syllable.

> by cry try dry

Notice the difference in spelling and pronunciation in the pairs of words below:

Short i	Long i
bit	bite
sit	site or sight
quit	quite
fin	fine
did	died
tip	type

2. *The Short and Long e Sounds*

The spelling of the "short *e* sound" /e/, as in *pet*, and the "long *e* sound" /iy/, as in *Pete*.

The "short *e* sound" is regularly spelled *e(c)*.

> met led fed ferry

The "short *e* sound" is often spelled *ea*.

> bread dead dread head weather
> heaven heavy measure wealth

Common exceptions are: says, said.

The "long *e* sound" /iy/, is regularly spelled *e(c)e*, *ee*, or *ea*.

> Pete concrete; meet feet; meat breathe

The letter *y* has the "long *e* sound" at the end of polysyllabic words like the following:

> happily merry healthy easy lovely

Notice the difference in spelling and pronunciation in the pairs of words below:

Short e	Long e
met	meet or meat
fed	feed
set	seat
bet	beet or beat
bread	breed
dead	deed
pet	Pete

3. *The Short And Long a Sounds*

The spelling of the "short *a* sound" /æ/, as in *pat*, and the "long *a* sound" /ey/, as in *tape*.

The "short *a* sound" /æ/, is regularly spelled *a(c)*,

> tap lack bath pass sad Sam can pal cap

The "long *a* sound" /ey/, is regularly spelled *a(c)e*, *ay*, *al*, *ey*, or *ei*.

tape lake bathe same cane pale; pay say play day;
sail mail pail; they convey; veil eight, neighbor vein.

Notice the difference in spelling and pronunciation in the pairs
of words below:

Short *a*	Long *a*
tap	tape
cap	cape
lack	lake
pass	pace
bath	bathe
pal	pale
at	ate or eight
van	vain, vein, or vane

4. *The Short And Long o sounds*

The spelling of the "short *o* sounds" /a/ as in *pot*, or /ɔ/
as in *dog*, and the "long *o* sound" /ow/ as in *know*.

The "short *o* sounds" /a/ or /ɔ/ are regularly spelled *o(c)*.

not rob cop smock fox cost long cloth office often

The "long *o* sound" is regularly spelled *o(c)e*, *oa*, *ow*, and *ou*.

note robe cope smoke;   boat coat throat soap;
bowl sow grow know;   soul shoulder

Notice the differences in spelling and pronunciation in the pairs of words below:

Short *o*	Long *o*
not	note
rob	robe
cop	cope
smock	smoke
fox	folks
cost	coast
cloth	clothe

5. *The Short And Long u Sounds And The Short oo Sound*

The spelling of the "short *u* sound" /ə/ as in *but*, the "long *u* sounds" /uw/ or /yuw/ as in *who* and *cute*, and the "short *oo* sound" /u/, as in *put*.

There is not really a regular spelling for the "short *u* sound" It is usually spelled *u(c)*, *ou*, or *o*.

> cut us tub run rush rub mud much luck; country double enough trouble rough tough; come some govern nothing other brother mother love glove done does month son front money

There are also several spellings for the "long *u* sounds". They are spelled *u(c)e* (or another vowel), *ew*, *ul*, or *o*.

> June July use usually music human; news knew few; fruit juice suit; who move prove

Other spellings are used in Tuesday beauty beautiful.

The /u/ sound, as in *took*, is spelled with *oo* (*c*) or *u(c)*.

> took cook book shook look good stood hood wood foot; put pull bull full bush push cushion butcher

6. *Spelling Of Vowel Sounds Followed By r*

Spelling of /ihr/ as in *here*, /ehr/ as in *air*, /ohr/ or /ɔhr/ as in *four*, /uhr/ as in *tour*, /ahr/ as in *part*, and /əhr/ as in *girl*.

/ihr/ is spelled *ear*, *eer*, or *ere*.

> ear clear dear fear; cheer beer queer career; merely here adhere interfere

/ehr/ is spelled *air*, *are*, *ear*, *ere*, or *eir*.

> air pair chair fair stairs; fare care share rare; wear bear pear tear; there where; their heir

/ohr/ and /ɔhr/ are spelled *or*, *oor*, *our*, or *ar*.

> or for; floor door; four pour; war warm

/uhr/ is spelled *ur(e)*, *oor*, *our*. *ur(e)* is usually pronounced /yuhr/.

> sure cure pure; poor boor; your tour

/ahr/ is regularly spelled *ar(c)*; sometimes *ear*.

> are March large car park farm; heart

/əhr/ is spelled *ur*, *ir*, *er*, *(w)or*, or *ear(c)*.

> burn turn hurry hurt; thirteen thirty girl sir first; her were person verb; work word worry world worth; heard earth learn earn

1. *Spelling Of Consonant Sounds*

The spelling of the consonant sounds in which one sound is regularly represented by one letter.

/b/	B	boy big; able horrible; job
/d/	D	date dime; ready older; bad good
/g/	G	game go; bigger cigarette; rug dig
/h/	H	hat health; behind anyhow
/l/	L	live leave; finally lately; will fill
/m/	M	might may; important grammar; home same
/p/	P	pay picture; happy apply; up cap
/t/	T	time terrible; little butter; ate at
/v/	V	very vegetable; every flavor; give have
/w/	W	will world; away anyway

2. *Spelling Of Consonant Sounds*

Spelling of the consonant sounds which are regularly represented by one of several letters, or a combination of letters.

/f/ F or PH	find found; awful careful; if off; philosophy; telephone; graph
/n/ N or KN or GN (rare)	nice near; many money; man men; knife know knowledge; gnat gnu
/r/ R or WR	read room; Mary wearing; car are; write wrote
/k/ C, K, CK	The letter *c* regularly represents /k/ before *a, o,* and *u,* and before *l* and *r*. cat cop cute; class clear; cream critical

The letter *k* has only one sound, /k/, and is
regularly used before *e* and *i*, after *l*, *n*
and *r*, with "long" vowels, and *oo*.
ck represents the /k/ in the middle or at the
end of words.
Ken kettle; kiss kill; milk silk; dark work;
thank ink; cheek leak soak break cake like
coke Luke look took; black deck block tick

/s/ S or C

The letter *s* represents two sounds, /s/, and
/z/. (See below.)

the letter *c* also represents two sounds, /k/
(See above) and /s/.
The letter *c* regularly represents the /s/
sound when it is used before *e* and *i*.
say see; sister missing; bus yes;
cell circle; recess placing; peace ice

/z/ Z or S

The letter *z* has only one sound, /z/. The
letter *s* has two sounds, /s/ at the beginning
of words, and /s/ or /z/ in the middle or at
the end of words.
zoo zero; fuzzy lazy; size prize;
easy busy; lose these

/j/ J or G

The letter *j* has only one sound and is used
at the beginning of words. *g* has two, /j/
and /g/.
g regularly represents /j/ before *e* and *i*.
(Common exceptions: get, give, girl and their
derivatives.)
jelly jam; George genius; raging ginger;
cage large

/š/ SH

The letters *sh* regularly represent the /š/
sound, but in the middle of words, the letters
ti often represent this sound.
shoe share; wishing cushion; dish fish
nation condition action fiction

/č/ CH

The letters *ch* regularly represent the /č/
sound, but in the middle of words, the letter

t often occurs instead.
church child; kitchen itching; each such
nature culture actual ritual

/θ/	TH	thin thanks; nothing something; breath birth

/ð/ TH   this that; mother father; bathe clothe

/y/ Y or U   (See 5. for *u* spellings.)
you your; beyond unyielding

/ŋ/ NG   This sound never occurs at the beginning
of English words.
singer ringing; thing long

/ž/ S or G   This sound never occurs at the beginning
of English words. In the middle of words,
it is usually represented by *s*(*v*), and at the
end of words by *g*(*v*).
measure vision; rouge garage

Note the following combinations of consonant sounds: /kw/
is regularly represented by the letters QU: quick quiet quite. In
the middle and at the end of words, /ks/ is sometimes represented by the letter X: Mexico excellent; tax box.

140